21, 22, 23, 30,
41, 42, 53, 70,
73. 87, 99, 134,
135, 147, 150-51
172, 202, 244,
256, 287-291
293-96

Victory!

**Applying the Proven Principles of
Military Strategy to Achieve Success
in Your Business and Personal Life**

Brian Tracy

AMACOM

American Management Association

New York • Atlanta • Brussels • Buenos Aires • Chicago • London • Mexico City
San Francisco • Shanghai • Tokyo • Toronto • Washington, D. C.

Special discounts on bulk quantities of AMACOM books are available to corporations, professional associations, and other organizations. For details, contact Special Sales Department, AMACOM, a division of American Management Association, 1601 Broadway, New York, NY 10019.
Tel.: 212-903-8316   Fax: 212-903-8083
Web site: *www.amacombooks.org*

This publication is designed to provide accurate and authoritative information in regard to the subject matter covered. It is sold with the understanding that the publisher is not engaged in rendering legal, accounting, or other professional service. If legal advice or other expert assistance is required, the services of a competent professional person should be sought.

Library of Congress Cataloging-in-Publication Data

Tracy, Brian.
    Victory!: applying the proven principles of military strategy to achieve greater success in your business and personal life / Brian Tracy.
        p. cm.
Includes index.
    ISBN 0-8144-0750-1
    1. Success—Psychological aspects. 2. Success in business. I. Title.

    BF637.S8 T637 2002
    650.1—dc21   2002008307

Printing number
10 9 8 7 6 5 4 3 2 1

This book is dedicated to Edwin J. Feulner, Jr., a dear friend, a fine executive, a great patriot, and a man who has done more to assure the victory of the American values of freedom, opportunity, prosperity, and civil society than perhaps anyone else alive.

Contents

Chapter Seven

Chapter Eight

Chapter Nine

Chapter Ten

Chapter Eleven

Chapter Twelve

Conclusion

Preface

From the time I was 15 years old, I have been fascinated by the military commanders who were able to achieve astounding victories against great odds, often far from home. There was even a rumor that Napoleon Bonaparte carried a copy of *The Art of War* by Sun Tzu on his campaigns and that this book was the secret to his successes in battle, making him one of the greatest generals in history.

In working with hundreds of companies and thousands of executives and entrepreneurs, I have found that exceptionally successful men and women often have qualities similar to those of the great military leaders through the ages. Like generals commanding armies, they also use proven and practical principles to achieve success against great odds and to achieve far more than those who do not know and apply these principles.

Results are the measure of effectiveness. But results alone are not enough; they must be attained in a timely fashion. Time is precious. It is invaluable, indispensable, irreplaceable, and necessary. It is the *stuff of life* and must be husbanded and used with great care.

The purpose of this book is to introduce you to many of the same ideas and strategies used by the most effective men and women in every field and to give you specific tools you can use to achieve victory in your personal and business life.

Just as the commander with the best soldiers, armaments, and matériel has a decided advantage over the opposing force, the individual who has the greatest arsenal of thinking tools will win out over the competition time and time again.

My goal for you in writing this book is to save you an enormous amount of time in achieving your most important goals.

In the pages ahead, I will present you with military principles and give you some of the best thinking tools ever discovered for achieving great success. You will then have them for the rest of your life, and you can use them to attain victory in everything you do, far faster than you ever would without them.

Introduction

Once upon a time, a young man from the Midwest was living in New York in a boarding house and working at a low-level job in a large company. He had come from an average background and had only a high school education. He had little confidence in himself or in his long-term ability to accomplish very much in life. For almost three years, he got up in the morning, went to work, did his job, socialized with his few friends, and just accepted that this is the way things were supposed to be.

One day, an elderly stranger moved into the boarding house. The older man had traveled widely and claimed not only to be able to tell fortunes but also to tell people who they had been in their previous lives. The young man and the stranger met and spoke regularly as they came and went to and from their daily routines. One day, the stranger sat down with the young man and told him that he had had a revelation about the young man's previous life, and that about these things he was never wrong.

He told the young man that in a previous life, he had been Napoleon Bonaparte. He had been one of the great statesmen, generals, and leaders of history. As Napoleon Bonaparte, he had risen from humble beginnings on the Island of Corsica, developed himself through hard work and application, become an officer in the French army, and eventually had risen to become Emperor of France.

The older man seemed to know of the young man's life as Napoleon in great detail. He went on to tell him that Napoleon Bonaparte had led his armies in hundreds of battles all over Europe and Egypt and had achieved incredible victories against overwhelming odds. He had completely transformed the government of France and gone down in history as one of the greatest leaders of all time.

The young man was extremely skeptical. He didn't really believe the stranger, even though he was flattered and intrigued by the idea of having been powerful and famous in a previous life. But as the weeks went by, the boarder kept adding new details about the young man's life as Napoleon Bonaparte and his qualities of leadership, character, and personality. Eventually, the stranger's wealth of detail and absolute conviction that the young man had actually been Napoleon in a previous life convinced the young man that the story was indeed true.

From that point forward, the young man began looking into himself for any indication that he might have the qualities of a great leader. He began to study the life and exploits of Napoleon. The more he studied Napoleon and the qualities of leadership, generalship, and the power of command Napoleon exerted over his armies, the more the young man noticed that he also had the same qualities deep within him.

He began to study other generals as well. He studied military history. He studied books on leadership, both in business and in warfare. Repeatedly, he noticed occasions when he exhibited many of the same qualities that leaders everywhere had demonstrated throughout history. And the more he thought about these qualities, the more he began to walk and talk like a leader in his work.

He volunteered for assignments and took on additional responsibilities. He spent his spare time studying and upgrading his skills. He took the initiative to solve problems, make decisions, and get things done at his company. He held nothing back. Bit by bit, his fears and doubts were replaced by confidence and courage.

His superiors noticed the changes in the young man. They began to give him tasks and responsibilities commensurate with his increasing competence. Each time he was given something more to do, the young man embraced the opportunity and threw himself wholeheartedly into doing the job in an excellent fashion. As a result, he became more knowledgeable and experienced. He was soon paid more and promoted repeatedly.

By the time he was thirty, he was a different person than when he had moved from the Midwest. He had completely transformed from a shy young man to a bold, confident executive. He made ever greater and more important contributions to his company. Eventually, he rose to the top of his field and became a leading figure in his industry.

Pushing to the Front

Whether or not this story is true doesn't matter. The lesson of the story is this: If you think and act like a leader—if you learn the qualities and behaviors of great leaders, and you apply them in your daily life—you will inevitably evolve and mature into a leadership position in whatever you do. By taking complete charge of your life and your future, you will put yourself onto the fast track in your career.

Throughout history, some of the finest examples of leadership have been shown by generals who achieved victory in chaotic situations, often against great odds. Often, the decision of a single officer at one critical moment has decided the outcome of a battle, and even the fate of an empire. The incredible stress and confusion of the clash of armies often brings out the very best in a person.

Modern life is a battle as well. You are constantly competing in your work and business against uncertain forces in a turbulent environment. You face a never-ending succession of problems and crises. And while soldiers only fight in a few battles during their lifetimes, your battles never end.

Our uncertain world needs leaders now more than at any other time in history. There is perhaps no better decision that you can make than to be a leader — in your work, your family, your community, and your personal life. Your job is to step forward and take command. Your job is to accept responsibility and get things done.

Your success in life is largely determined by your ability to get results, to follow through in the face of adversity. The more difficult, the more important, the results you achieve, the greater the glory and rewards you receive for achieving them.

The quality of your life is determined by the quality of your thinking. The better you think, the better results you get. The more you identify with and emulate leaders, both past and present, the more you become like them. The more you think like a leader, the more you take the actions that leaders take and the more you get the results that leaders get.

Military Leaders Over the Centuries

Over the centuries, we have studied great military leaders and analyzed their battles. Thousands of historians and researchers have devoted themselves to finding the common denominators of victory or defeat in warfare. They have concluded that successful commanders win largely because of boldness, speed, surprise, and resolute determination to achieve victory.

From the days of Thucydides and his *History of the Peloponnesian War*, the core principles of military strategy have been identified. These principles have then been taught to subsequent generations of officers in the armed services and military schools worldwide.

There are *twelve* basic principles of military strategy, which are necessary to assure victory and to avoid defeat. Each one of these principles by itself has been responsible for victories or defeats. Each of them is as applicable to business and personal success as to warfare.

These twelve principles, around which this book is written, are the Principles of the Objective, the Offensive, the Mass, Maneuver, Intelligence, Concerted Action, Unity of Command, Simplicity, Security, Economy, Surprise, and Exploitation. In a tight contest, violation of any one of these principles can lead to defeat

Your goal as an entrepreneur, executive, sales professional, parent, employee, committee member—whatever you endeavor— is to learn and practice these principles in your business. This book will show you how you can apply each one of these strategic thinking concepts to getting better results, faster, perhaps, than you ever imagined possible. They will show you how to achieve victory!

The Use of Force Multipliers

The twelve principles of military strategy explain most victories and every defeat, success, or failure—on the battlefield or in business or personal life. In addition, there are *force multipliers*, which can dramatically change the odds and improve the likelihood of victory or success in any competitive situation. A force multiplier enables a smaller force to increase its hitting power and impact at a critical point where victory is possible.

By applying one or more force multipliers to your situation, you can gain an advantage that enables you to defeat your enemy or outperform your competition. Some of these force multipliers are:

- Superior knowledge

- Greater skill

- Optimism

- Confidence

- High morale

- Creativity and innovation

- The ability to focus and concentrate on key targets and objectives

- Strategic alliances

- Excellent relationships with key people and organizations

- Excellent communications among all people involved

- Superior leadership at all levels

These are all factors that you can develop and apply to your business and personal life. How many of them do you use already?

Your Future Is Unlimited

Each of the principles of military strategy can be learned, and each of the force multipliers can be developed, thereby enabling you to multiply your own effectiveness and that of your organization.

Just as young officers are taught to think and take actions consistent with these principles and force multipliers in the various military academies, you can learn and practice these principles in the rough and tumble of daily life.

In your personal and work life, the stakes may not be as high as they are on the battlefield, where life and death hangs in the balance. Nevertheless, men and women who achieve great things are those who take their responsibilities and their situations seriously. They leave nothing to chance. They study and prepare themselves so that they are ready to perform consistently well in the critical battles and key moments of life and work.

Your goal is not just to make a living, but also to make a great life. Your goal is to fulfill your potential as a person, in every area, and to become everything that you are capable of becoming over the course of your life and career. As the army recruiting poster says, "Be all that you can be." And to paraphrase famous Green Bay Packer coach Vince Lombardi, "Winning is not a one-time thing; it's an all-the-time thing."

The great mistake that most people make is not realizing one key point: The failure to commit to excellence, to victory, leads by default to the subconscious acceptance of mediocrity and eventual defeat.

This book is written for the ambitious, energetic, determined, success-oriented individual, from executives, entrepreneurs, professionals, and other business leaders to leaders of

all descriptions in all walks of life, who are absolutely determined to win big in life and work.

In the pages ahead, you will learn how to apply each of
these key military principles of strategy in everything you do.
You will learn how to think and plan strategically, focus and
concentrate your talents and resources, take advantage of
opportunities, protect against setbacks, work more effectively
with others, and maximize all your abilities to achieve extraordinary success. You will learn how to achieve personal victory
in whatever you choose. You will learn how to win the key battles, the ones that really matter. You will learn how to accomplish more in the next couple of years than most people
accomplish in a lifetime of work.

CHAPTER ONE

The Principle of the Objective
Clarity Is Essential

Pursue one great decisive aim with force and determination...

— MAJOR GENERAL KARL VON CLAUSEWITZ

In every war, every battle, every great human endeavor, there must be clear, specific goals and objectives. Each person who is responsible for a part of the result must know exactly what that result is and how it is to be measured. The greater the degree of clarity, the more likely it is that the goal will be achieved.

The Battle of Arbela

On the first of October in 331 B.C., a battle between the well-rested, veteran troops of Alexander and the tired soldiers in the army of the Persian King Darius III would decide the fate of an empire. Alexander had allowed some of his scouts to be captured and interrogated. They told Darius III that Alexander was planning a night attack. Darius therefore kept his entire army awake and in full battle formation all night. To reinforce this perception, Alexander sent light skirmishing forces in a series of quick attacks on the flanks of the Persian army, darting in and out, throughout the night. On the other side of the Plain of Gaugamela, near the town of Arbela on the Tigris in Assyria, the Macedonian army had retired early and slept well. The fatigue of the Persians was, however, only one factor that Alexander counted on for victory.

The Persian army definitely had the advantage in the sense that they outnumbered Alexander's army. From the numerous accounts of this battle by ancient Greek historians such as Arrian and from Plutarch's *Life of Alexander the Great*, we know that the strength of the Persian army was about 200,000 men. Alexander had an army of less than 50,000 infantry and cavalry under his command. The Persians would only have to extend their front and sweep around both flanks to crush the Macedonians once and for all. Alexander had already defeated them in two previous battles, and the Persians were eager for revenge.

When the sun rose on the Plain of Gaugamela, the entire Macedonian army was drawn up at an oblique angle, with cavalry at either end of the formation, and with the heavy infantry (the phalanx, the shield-bearers, and the hoplites) in formation in the center. As always, Alexander rode his great black warhorse Bucephalus and wore a shining, jewel-encrusted helmet above a flowing red cape so that everyone in his army, and in the enemy army, could see him clearly.

Darius launched his assault on the outnumbered Macedonians by sending forward his 300 battle chariots with razor-like scythes spinning on the axles. Alexander had anticipated this initial assault and immediately ordered his javelin throwers forward to hurl wave after wave of deadly accurate javelins into the oncoming horses and men. The chariots, horses, and riders were torn to pieces by the oncoming missiles and were quickly eliminated as an effective fighting force.

Meanwhile, the cavalry on either flank of Darius's army attacked the right and left flanks of the Macedonian army. A bitter fight ensued. But the well-disciplined Macedonian center held firm and began moving right, toward the left flank of the Persian army.

As the Persian front shifted sideways to counter the movement of the Macedonians, a hole opened up in the center of the Persian line. Alexander, seeing his opportunity, gave a loud battle cry and with his companion guard of elite cavalry pursued Darius himself.

Alexander led the attack. His men, the finest fighting cavalry in the world, hurtled after him. They carved through the front of the Persian line like a knife through butter, heading directly toward Darius's command post in the center of the army.

Alexander's objective was clear from the beginning. He knew that the Persian army was made up of conscripted troops from all over the empire. They were not loyal to each other; they were only loyal to Darius, the king. Alexander was certain that if he could kill Darius or drive him from the field, the remaining troops would not stand and fight for each other. Alexander's military philosophy was that the opposing general in command was the linchpin that held the enemy army together. He planned each battle to create an opportunity where he could launch his elite cavalry, like a spear, at the enemy general in the middle of the army. In every case, when the enemy general was killed or driven to flight, the rest of the army would lose its cohesion and begin to disintegrate. Victory quickly followed.

As Alexander and his elite cavalry formed a wedge that cut through the front of the Persian army toward Darius, the king lost his nerve, leaped on a horse, and fled from the battlefield. His subordinate generals immediately jumped on their horses and followed him. The word traveled like wildfire throughout the Persian army, "The Macedonians are in the center, and Darius has fled. The battle must be lost. Run for it!"

Without leadership, the army started to come apart. There were two more hours of bitter fighting, between the Persian and Macedonian cavalry on the flanks, and the Persian and Macedonian troops in the center. But the Macedonians under Alexander prevailed. It was a defeat, then a rout, then a slaughter. By the end of the day, the Persians are believed to have lost about 90,000 men. The Macedonian dead numbered only about 500. This victory made Alexander the master of Persia, at that time the greatest empire in the world. He was twenty-five years old.

Alexander was perhaps the greatest military commander in history, a leader who was never defeated on the battlefield. One of the reasons for his successes was his absolute clarity about the objective to be achieved in each battle.

THE PRINCIPLE OF THE OBJECTIVE: Direct all efforts toward a clearly defined, decisive, and attainable objective.

The ultimate goal of war is the fulfillment of the policy for which the war is being fought. The accomplishment of this goal often requires the defeat of the enemy's armed forces and of the destruction of his means or will to resist. The principle of the objective is applicable at all echelons. Goals of smaller units are frequently altered in campaigns and wars, but seldom in the midst of battle.

Make It Clear and Simple

When General Dwight D. Eisenhower was sent by General George C. Marshall to take command of the allied forces in London in World War II, his orders and his objective were clear: "Proceed to London. Invade Europe. Defeat the Germans."

When General Norman Schwarzkopf was dispatched to command the allied forces against Iraq in the Gulf War in 1991, his orders were also clear: "Get the Iraqi army out of Kuwait."

The air forces that provided cover to the army in the Gulf had a single objective with regard to the Iraqi air force: "If it flies, it dies."

In warfare, as in all areas of life, the objective must have five qualities. It must be:

1. **Clear.** The objective must be absolutely clear to all those who are expected to be instrumental in attaining it. When the goal is to seize a specific objective, each person responsible must know what the objective is, where it is, and when it is to be seized.

2. **Attainable.** The objective should be realistic and within the span of control of the unit to which it is assigned. The goal should not require superhuman strengths or abilities, and it must be attainable with the resources of the unit assigned to that goal.

3. Decisive. The objective must be significant and meaningful and must make a worthwhile contribution to the achievement of higher-order objectives. Lives should not be risked to attain an objective that is not essential to the success of the overall campaign.

4. Specific. The objective should be measurable; it should be expressed in such a way that it is clear whether or not it has been accomplished. A third party should be able to judge whether or not the objective has been attained.

5. Time-bounded. There must be a specific deadline along with time lines for the achievement of the objective. A specific date and time must be given for the attainment of a clear, decisive, and specific objective.

Clear objectives, backed by detailed plans, vigorously executed with boldness and persistence, lead to success time and time again. Unclear or fuzzy objectives, often accompanied by confusing or contradictory plans, lead to underachievement and defeat over and over.

The Principle of the Objective in Business

The same principles that apply to the achievement of military battle objectives also apply to the achievement of business goals in competitive markets. You must know exactly how much of what product or service is to be sold, by whom, at what price, to which customer group, and how it is to be paid for, produced, and delivered. In every case, the most important word is *clarity*. The greater your clarity regarding exactly what it is you are trying to accomplish, the greater the likelihood that you will achieve it on schedule.

Strategic planning in warfare is analogous to strategic business planning and to personal strategic planning. Success in any area of life is a direct result of knowing exactly what you want and then determining the very best way to achieve it. When you have a clear target to aim at, and you have carefully planned every step of the way to your goal, you will accomplish vastly more in a shorter period of time than if you started off without a clear strategic plan. Almost everything we talk about in this book can be used in either area of your life to increase your effectiveness and to improve the quality and quantity of the results that you accomplish.

Idealization

Begin setting objectives for your business or your company's business by projecting forward three to five years and imagining a *perfect* future. Decide what is right before you decide what is possible. If the business were ideal in every respect five years from today, what would it look like?

Imagine that you could wave a magic wand and create the perfect situation in every part of the company. Imagine that you have all the money, manpower, and resources to do anything you want in your organization. If the business were perfect in five years, what would be its level of sales, profitability, and reputation in the marketplace? How much would your company be earning, and what would your *personal* income be?

All business planning begins with an ideal vision of the future. Clarifying and sharing this vision is a key responsibility of leadership. As the Bible says, "Where there is no vision, the people perish." Where there is no vision in a company, people are eventually reduced to simply going through the motions, operating from day to day, with no idea of the kind of future they are supposed to be creating.

Company Objectives

The purpose of a business strategy is to provide a plan to organize and deploy the resources of the business in such a way as to increase the *return on equity* invested in the business. This is the amount of money that the owners of the business have put at risk to earn a profit.

The second aim of business strategy is to *decrease costs* by finding better, faster, cheaper ways to produce the same products or services and accomplish the same results.

The third objective of business strategy is to identify and exploit the opportunities of tomorrow while simultaneously reducing the risks of today.

There are four key questions with regard to setting objectives that you should ask and answer continually, especially when you are experiencing resistance or frustration of any kind in the accomplishment of your goals. These questions are:

1. **What are we trying to do?** What exactly are your goals? Are they written down, clear, specific, time-bounded, and measurable? Lack of clarity with regard to goals leads to lack of accomplishment, both in the short term and in the long term.

2. **How are we trying to do it?** Always remain open to the possibility that there could be a different or better way to accomplish the same objective—with lower costs, lower risks, and greater certainty.

3. **What are our assumptions?** What are you assuming about your current situation that may not be true at all? Every decision is made on the basis of certain assumptions, either clear or unclear. As Alex MacKenzie, author of *The Time Trap,* wrote, "Errant assumptions lie at the root of every failure." For example, in World War II, the fortress of Singapore was supposedly impregnable, but the British defenders assumed that any attack on Singapore would come from the sea. When the Japanese instead attacked from the landward side to the north, the British were quickly overwhelmed and surrendered a garrison of 62,000 men on February 15, 1942. Winston Churchill described it as, "The worst disaster and largest capitulation in British history."

4. **What if our assumptions are wrong?** What if you are taking actions today that would be completely inappropriate for achieving your objectives if certain assumptions were wrong? Always be open to the possibility that you are *dead wrong* in your beliefs and assumptions. If you were wrong, what changes would you have to make immediately to survive and thrive in your current market?

The GOSPA Model of Strategic Planning

There is a simple five-step formula that you can use for establishing clear objectives and for strategic planning for the rest of your career. As regularly as breathing in and breathing out, you should practice these five principles in every part of your business.

Step One. The first letter, "G," stands for *Goals.* Goals in business represent the final financial results that you want to achieve. All business goals can be defined in financial terms. Your goals must be clear, written, and specific. They must be measurable and exact. They must be time-bounded with deadlines.

Some examples of financial goals are sales volume, net profit, return on equity, return on investment, return on sales, growth rate, market share, and profit per customer. Which numbers you choose to zero in on largely determines how you will organize and deploy the people and resources of your business.

Step Two. The second letter, "O," stands for *Objectives*. In this case, your objectives are the subgoals that you must accomplish to achieve your larger, final goals. Some of the subgoals that you will have to accomplish before you can achieve your larger goals of profitability and return on investment are the following:

1. You must obtain, organize, and deploy the necessary financial resources to build and maintain your business operation.

2. You must acquire, train, manage, and motivate the appropriate people to do the job and carry out the work.

3. You will have to advertise, promote, market, and sell a specific volume of products or services within a specific time, at specific prices, yielding specific levels of profit.

4. Once you have accomplished the first three goals, you will have to produce, manufacture, distribute, and deliver the products and services that you have sold.

5. You will have to organize the logistical and administrative details of the business in order to handle the information, paperwork, processing, and other activities that underpin all successful business enterprise.

Once your goals and objectives are clear to you, and to everyone you depend upon to carry them out, you can move on to step 3 in the GOSPA Model.

Step Three. The third letter, "S," stands for *Strategies*. These are the different approaches or ways that you can go about achieving your goals and objectives. To get from Point A to Point B, there are many different routes you can follow. Your choice of an appropriate strategy will largely determine whether or not you succeed or fail. The choice of the correct strategy is therefore vitally important.

Begin by asking this question: "What are all the different ways that we can accomplish this goal?" Remember, a goal not yet achieved is merely a problem not yet solved. Approach the attainment of a goal or an objective as you would seek the solution to a problem. For example, Alexander approached his battles by answering the question, "How can I undermine the objectives and morale of the enemy's army?" He succeeded by making the enemy believe its goal was unattainable. Remain open to different and unusual solutions.

Beware of any goal or objective for which there is only one possible strategy. Beware of any problem for which there is only one solution. Beware of any question for which there is only one answer. Continue asking the question, *"What else could be the answer?"* Before you finalize a strategy, you should have a variety of potential strategies available to you. This requires the hard work of *thinking* and is the key responsibility of the leader and the decision-maker.

Once you have developed a series of possible strategies or approaches to achieving your goal or solving your problem, you should evaluate each of these options based on the following factors:

1. What are your capabilities? Just because you *want* to do something does not mean that you are capable of doing it. Desire and enthusiasm are wonderful qualities, but they do not translate into effective results unless they are accompanied by core competencies and capabilities.

In Jim Collins's 2001 book *From Good to Great*, he makes the key point that the great companies are those that put the right people in place, in the key positions, before they make any final decisions about goals, objectives, and strategy. Do you have the people you need? Can you get them? The most effective fighting forces have the best trained and most aggressive officers at all levels.

2. Do you have the resources, both internal and external, to carry out a particular strategy? General Bernard Law Montgomery, known as "Martini Montgomery," was obsessive about having far greater supplies of weapons, armament, and matériel than he would need before launching a major attack against the enemy. This was the key to his victory at El Alamein over Field Marshal Erwin Rommel in 1942. Do you have the necessary financial resources? Do you have the necessary contacts and alliances in the marketplace? Do you have the necessary knowledge, skill, and experience to carry out a particular strategy? If not, can you acquire them? If you cannot get them, what would be an alternate strategy that is more consistent with the resources that you have available? These are key questions that you must ask and answer before you commit to a particular course of action.

3. What is the situation in the marketplace today? Are sales for your product or service strong or weak? Are sales growing or declining? Are the trends in the market moving in your favor and boosting your sales and profitability, or are the trends moving against you? A good leader is very sensitive to the nuances of the environment and is constantly testing his assumptions about the state of business as it actually exists today.

4. Who is your competition, and how are they likely to react to any strategy of yours? In Michael Porter's book *Competitive Advantage*, he emphasizes the importance of considering the responses of your competitors to any action you take in the market. There is a military axiom: "No strategy ever survives first contact with the enemy." You must carefully plan every possible detail of your strategy and logistics. But you must be prepared to modify your strategy quickly in response to unexpected actions taken by your competitors to defend their markets or to seize yours.

Whatever your strategy, you should assume that your competitors will move to counteract it in some way. The more successful you are with your strategy in making sales and taking market share, the more vigorously and aggressively your competitors will move to either copy your strategy or undermine your perceived strengths. Therefore, whatever strategy you decide upon, keep your plans to yourself as long as possible. When you do launch, aim to get there "firstest with the mostest" so that you can achieve maximum results before your competition reacts.

Count Otto von Bismarck, the "Iron Chancellor" of Germany, was considered to be the foremost diplomat and statesman of his time. He was famous for always having a "Plan B," a "Bismarck Plan," in his drawer. This was his fallback plan in case his first plan did not work. No matter what happened, no matter what reverses he experienced at the great councils of Europe, he was always ready to bounce back with a well-developed and well-thought-out alternative plan.

You should do the same. Once you have decided upon a particular strategy, you should immediately develop an alternate strategy, just in case the first strategy doesn't work. Having an alternative plan to fall back on gives you a greater sense of confidence, courage, and boldness in executing your original plan. It is a powerful psychological factor that you should use to your advantage.

Step Four. The fourth letter in GOSPA, "P," stands for *Plans.* Your plans are the rungs on the ladder from where you are to wherever it is you want to go. The planning stage is where the rubber meets the road. This is the *real* key to your success. As Patton said, "Take plenty of time to set up an attack. It takes at least two hours to prepare an infantry battalion to execute a properly coordinated attack. Shoving them in too soon produces useless losses."

"In war, nothing is achieved by calculation. Everything that is not soundly planned in its details yields no results."

Begin the planning process by making a list of every single thing that you will have to do to achieve your goal or objective. Leave nothing out. Be as detailed as you can. When you think of a new task or activity, write it down on the list. Keep working on this list until it is complete in every detail and describes the process of achievement from the first step to the final victory.

Next, make a list of everything that you will need in order to carry out every activity in your plan. List the people, knowledge, and skills that you will require. List the furniture, fixtures, and facilities that you will need. List the financial resources that will be necessary. Remember, "The devil is in the details." The most effective leaders, like the most effective military commanders, are those who think through every detail in advance and never trust to luck for anything.

Once you have your lists of activities and resources, organize these lists in two ways:

1. Organize your activities by *priority.* Which items are more important, and which are less important? Use the 80/20 Rule. What are the 20 percent of your activities that will account for 80 percent of the value of all of your activities? Use the ABC Method of setting priorities. "A" priorities are very important. There are serious consequences if they are not done in a timely fashion. "B" activities are those that should be done, but they are not as important as "A" activities. "C" activities are things that would be *nice* to do, but they are not as important as "A" or "B" activities.

Your ability to analyze your list of activities and assign correct priorities to them is a critical skill of both success and leadership. It is often the determining factor between success and failure.

2. Organize your list in terms of the *time* at which the tasks must be completed. Something may be very important, a top priority, but it may not be required for several weeks or months. Every activity has a specific time/date requirement. Each of these tasks should be in order and then combined with your priorities to create your finished plan.

Determine which activities are *parallel* and can be done simultaneously with other activities. Many things can be done

at the same time at which other things are being done. You can
dramatically increase the speed at which you accomplish a goal
by having several people or organizations working on different
parts of the business.

When World War II began, the U.S. Navy was woefully short
of ships to transport men and supplies to Britain. Henry J.
Kaiser was assigned by the war department to build "Liberty
Ships" as quickly as possible to replace the large number of
ships that were being sunk by the German U-boats.

"The very worst use of time is to do something well that need not be done at all."

—BENJAMIN TREGOE

When Kaiser took over, it was taking two years to build and
launch a single ship. Within a year, he had reduced the building time to two months per ship. And in one incredible display
of American ingenuity and workmanship, he built a complete
Liberty Ship, ready for commission, in four days!

What Henry J. Kaiser and others found was that the planning
and pursuit of parallel activities enabled huge tasks to be completed in a fraction of the time that would be required if each
task was only started after an earlier task had been completed.

Finally, there are *sequential* activities. These are activities
that depend upon each other. One cannot be done before the

other is finished. It is almost always sequential activities that determine how fast you can finish a job, initiate a strategy, achieve a goal, or accomplish a final objective.

Identify the key sequential activities in your project-planning, and make sure that you get started on them early enough so that they do not hold up completion of the entire task.

Step Five. The final letter in GOSPA, "A," stands for *Activities*. These are the tasks that have to be completed to fulfill the plans. Your job, either managing yourself or managing others, is to be absolutely clear about the specific activities that need to be done every single day to carry out the strategy.

In working with others, practice *management by objectives.* Take the time to explain, discuss, and agree on the job or jobs to be done. Make sure that everyone knows how he or she will be measured and when the tasks are supposed to be completed. Encourage people to report to you if they are behind schedule. Keep in regular touch with them to make sure that they are accomplishing the required objectives as agreed.

Another way to manage activities is to practice *management by responsibility.* You can use this method with people whom you know and trust and who have demonstrated a certain level of proven competence. To get the most out of this method, you should delegate both authority and responsibility for the completion of the task. Set deadlines and subdeadlines so that the other person knows when the task is expected. Be available to help and support the other person if he runs into any problems or obstructions.

Finally, when you manage by *objectives* or manage by *responsibility*, remember that delegation is not abdication. Always inspect what you expect. The more vital the task is to the final objective, the more important it is that you stay on top of it. Never assume that things will get done without your regular and continued intervention and involvement. Like a doctor with a critically ill patient, you should make regular "spot checks" on your key staff to be sure that everything is on track and on schedule.

Business Objectives Are Market Objectives

In business, all strategic planning is market planning. The customer is not only king, the customer must be the center point of all thinking and planning in the setting and achieving of business goals. What the customer wants, what the customer needs, what the customer likes, what the customer dislikes, what the customer will pay for, and what the customer is being offered by your competitors are the critical factors that determine profits or losses, success or failure, especially in tough, competitive markets.

As Dun and Bradstreet concluded after fifty years of studying businesses of all kinds, the entirety of business wisdom can be summarized in one statement: "Businesses succeed because of *high* sales; businesses fail because of *low* sales. All else is commentary."

Having built, run, or managed twenty-two different companies, my philosophy has always been to concentrate on sales. Whenever you have financial problems of any kind, think exclusively in terms of making more sales and generating more revenues. Cash flow is king. The ability to generate the top line is the decisive ability in modern business.

In a recent survey, corporate executives were asked, "How important are sales to your organization?" Virtually every executive replied that sales were *extremely* important, if not the *most* important element in their businesses.

The executives were then asked, "How much of your time do you spend on sales- and marketing-related issues?" The average amount of time spent by business owners and executives turned out to be approximately 11 percent! All the rest was consumed by non-sales activities.

A business cannot "cost-cut" or save its way to success. The only way to survive and thrive in any market is to focus intensively and exclusively on producing and selling products and services that people are willing to buy and pay for and that make a profit for the company.

Sales Strategy Analyses

In strategic planning for organizations, consider the core questions in sales and marketing: "*What* is to be sold, to *whom*, and by *whom*, and *how*, and at *what price*, and *how* is it to be *delivered* and *paid* for?"

The failure to ask and answer these questions accurately is the primary cause for declining revenues and cash flow, and often the failure of the enterprise. The ability to ask and answer these questions correctly is the primary reason for business success.

Here are the key questions that a salesperson, business owner, or sales executive must ask and answer repeatedly:

1. **Who is our customer?** Define your ideal customer in terms of age, education, income, position, tastes, experience, background, and psychology. What are the trends? Who will be your customers of tomorrow? What do you need to do to make your products and services more appealing to your ideal customer?

2. **What does my customer consider value?** What is your customer willing to pay for in a competitive mar-

ket? What benefits does she expect to get from doing business with you? Of all the benefits that you offer, what is the most important benefit that the customer must be convinced that she will receive before she will make a buying decision? If you don't know the answer to this question, you need to go back to the drawing board.

3. **Who are my competitors?** What are all the different businesses (or alternative uses for the same money) that compete with you? Since customers can only purchase a limited number of products or services, who else is trying to acquire your same customer, and what are they doing differently from you?

4. **Why do my prospective customers buy from my competitors?** What benefits do they perceive in dealing with my competitors? What is it that they like about my competitors that causes them to prefer my competitors' offerings to my offerings?

5. **What is my competitive advantage?** What is it that we do better than anyone else? What is our unique selling proposition? Every successful business is built around a unique competitive advantage that no other competitor can offer. What is yours? What should it be? What could it be? This is a key question for business success.

6. **What do we need to do differently to attract more customers in the future?** Remember, whatever got you to where you are today is not enough to keep you there. What do you have to do better, faster, or cheaper to win the customers of tomorrow away from your competi-

tors? Your ability to answer this question accurately determines your business future.

7. **What is your value offering?** If past customers were to be interviewed, what would they say about you? How would they describe you? What words would they use to describe your products or services or their experiences in dealing with you? Most important, how could you influence your customers of the future so that they think and talk about you in the way that would be most helpful to you in a competitive marketplace?

Sales are the lifeblood of the business. "Nothing happens until a sale takes place." Whatever your position in your business, you are still in *sales*. Everything that you do contributes either to the making of a sale or to the fulfilling of a sale. The greater the impact you can have on sales and profitability, the more valuable you become. And the more you think about marketing, sales, and profitability, the more likely it is that you will do the critical things that improve those functions in your organization.

Personal Strategic Planning

The principle of the objective in military terms is to seize critical positions, take ground, and win battles and wars. The principle of the objective applied to business is to create and keep customers, to make profits, and to thrive in a competitive marketplace. The principle of the objective in *personal* terms refers to your ability to decide exactly what you really want in life, to make plans to achieve your goals, and then to carry out your plans in a timely fashion.

Your ability to set goals for yourself is the master skill of success. People who set clear goals for themselves and who know exactly what they want always accomplish vastly more, and accomplish it faster, than people who are not sure who they are or where they are going. The very act of setting goals transforms your life and virtually guarantees your future.

In goal setting, you always begin with the process of *idealization*. In study after study of high-performing men and women, the most successful people allow themselves to dream on a regular basis. They project forward five and ten years into the future and imagine what their perfect lives would look like if they were to achieve all their goals.

Imagine that you could get into a time machine and, in the blink of an eye, arrive at a point five years in the future. When you open your eyes, something miraculous has happened! *Your life is perfect in every way*. Every part of your home, family, and work life is ideal in every respect. Here is the question: "What does it look like?"

If your life were perfect in every way, what would it look like? This ability to define and describe your perfect future life is the key to setting goals for yourself in the present. Once you have defined your ideal perfect life, ask yourself, "What would have to have happened for this perfect life to become a reality?" I like to call this "Thinking in the *past perfect future subjunctive*." It is the highest form of speculative and creative thinking. It is the key to designing your own future.

Look around you in the present and practice idealization as well. Decide what you really want before you start thinking about all the reasons why it may not be possible. Imagine that you could wave a magic wand and be, do, and have everything and anything you wanted, without limitation. What goals would you set for yourself?

Imagine that you had freed a genie from a magic lamp, and the genie offered you three wishes, large or small, short-term or long-term. What would be your three wishes? Write them down.

Most people, when given three wishes or goals to write down, usually write a health goal, a relationship goal, and a financial goal. This is because health, relationships, and money represent the "golden triangle" of personal success and happiness. What are yours?

The Seven Vital Areas of Life

For you to be completely happy and live a balanced life, you need to set and achieve goals in seven areas. At each stage of your life, one or more of these areas will be of primary importance to you. If you are out of work, your career will be more important than anything else. If you have no relationship or an unhappy relationship, your relationship goals will take precedence over all others. If you are broke, your financial goals will be preeminent. The intensity of your need for various goals changes as your situation changes.

1. Career and Business: These are your goals for your work life. They include the work that you would most like to do, the kind of money you would like to earn, the skills and abilities you will require, the successes that you are striving toward, and your vision of your perfect work life sometime in the future.

The clearer you are about your answers to these questions, the faster you will achieve these goals.

2. Family and Relationships: According to Dr. Sidney Jourard, 85 percent of your happiness (or unhappiness) will be determined by your relationships. Even though these goals may be emotional and intangible, you should write them out, exactly as you would plan a financial or career goal.

What sort of relationship would make you the happiest? What kind of a family life do you want to have? What do you want to accomplish for and with your family? What would you like to change in your family and your relationships? What should you be doing more or less of to enjoy a better family life? If you could wave a magic wand over your family and relationships, what would you like to be different from the way it is today?

3. Money and Investments: What are your financial goals, short-term and long-term? How much do you want to earn? How much do you want to be worth when you retire? What are your income goals for the next three, five, and ten years? What will you have to do differently today in order to achieve your financial goals of the future?

4. Health and Fitness: What are your health and fitness goals? How much do you want to weigh? How much do you need to exercise each day and each week? How many hours per night do you want to sleep? How many days or weeks of vacation do you want each year? Especially, how long do you want to live, and what will you have to do, starting today, to make it more likely that you live that long?

5. Personal and Professional Development: Identify the critical knowledge and skills that you will need, both personally and professionally, to lead your field in the months and years ahead. What books will you have to read? What additional courses and seminars will you have to attend in order to upgrade your skills and abilities to enjoy the kind of life that is possible for you?

6. **Social and Community:** What kind of a difference do you want to make in your world? What do you want to do for your community? What social, religious, political, or other groups do you believe in and support? What sort of activities do you want to be more involved in to help make your world a better place?

7. **Inner Peace and Spiritual Development:** The greatest human good is *peace of mind*. Identify the times in your life when you have felt the very happiest. What gives you the greatest peace of mind today? What would have to happen for you to feel wonderful about your life? If you could wave a magic wand and create your ideal calendar or lifestyle, what would it look like?

Only 3 percent of adults have clear, written, specific goals. Your aim should be to join this top 3 percent. These people earn five and ten times as much as the average. They experience a much greater sense of control and much greater feelings of happiness and accomplishment than average people do. The very act of setting goals changes not only your body chemistry, but also your entire attitude toward yourself and your life.

How To Set and Achieve Goals

There is a powerful seven-step process that you can use to set and achieve any goal you can imagine for yourself. As Napoleon Hill, author of *Think and Grow Rich*, wrote, "Whatever the mind of man can conceive and believe, it can achieve."

Step One. Decide exactly what you want in each area of your life and then write it down in clear, specific language. Writing your goals on paper moves you into the top 3 percent of living adults.

Step Two. Set a deadline on your goal; if necessary, set sub-deadlines so that you can always measure how well you are doing and how fast you are moving toward what is most important to you.

Step Three. Identify all the problems and obstacles that stand between you and your goal. Select the biggest obstacle or road-block and make a plan to deal with it or remove it as soon as possible.

Step Four. Identify the people, groups, and organizations whose help or cooperation you will require to achieve your goal. Determine what they might accomplish by helping you. Anyone who wants to achieve large goals must have the help and support of many other people. Who are they?

Step Five. Identify the additional knowledge and skills that you will need to achieve your goal. Remember, as Les Brown, author of *Live Your Dreams*, says, "To achieve something you have never achieved before, you must become someone you have never been before." Select the one skill that can help you the most in the achievement of your biggest goal, and make a plan to acquire that skill as soon as possible.

Step Six. Take the answers to the first five steps and organize them into a plan of action. Make a list of every step that you will have to take to achieve your goal. Organize the list by priority and sequence. Organize parallel activities and sequential activities. Put time lines on each part of your plan. Commit the entire plan to writing and review it regularly.

Step Seven. Take action on your plan immediately. Do something every day that moves you in the direction of your most important goal. Never miss a day. As Robert Schuller said, "By the yard, it's hard; but inch by inch, anything's a cinch."

Getting Started

Take a sheet of paper and make a list of every goal that you would like to accomplish in the next three to five years, exactly as if you had no limitations at all. Imagine for the moment that you have all the time, all the money, all the friends, all the knowledge, all the skills, all the talents, all the resources, and all the opportunities that you require. Let your mind float freely. Then write down everything that you can think of having, being, or doing if your life and resources were unlimited.

This list can often run to fifty or a hundred goals, Once you have completed this list, go over the list and ask this magic question: "What one goal on this list, if I accomplished it, would have the greatest positive impact on my life?"

There is almost always one goal, usually a financial goal, that, if accomplished, would have more of an impact on your other goals than any other single goal. Once you have identified your most important goal, your *major definite purpose,* write it on a separate sheet of paper.

Then, set a deadline for achieving it and identify the obstacles standing in your way. Determine the people whose help and cooperation you will require, and identify the additional knowledge and skills that you will need. Combine your answers into a plan and then take action on your plan. Resolve from this moment on that you will do something every day to move you toward the achievement of your major definite purpose.

When you start working every day toward clear, written goals, you will be amazed at how fast your life will change for the better, and how rapidly you will start moving toward your goals.

Perhaps the most important outwardly identifiable quality of the high performer or leader in every area is *action orientation*. Men and women who accomplish great things are invariably proactive rather than reactive. They take charge and take command of their lives and of the goals and objectives of their organizations. They become moving targets. They are constantly in motion. They work harder and faster than anyone else and, as a result, they accomplish vastly more than anyone else.

The Principle of the Objective Revisited

Resolve today, no matter what you are doing at the moment, to develop absolute clarity about your objectives in every part of your life. You can't hit a target that you can't see. The greater clarity you develop with regard to your goals and objectives, the more rapidly you will accomplish them. You will become unstoppable!

CHAPTER TWO

The Principle of the Offensive
Dare to Go Forward

War, once declared, must be waged offensively, aggressively.
The enemy must not be fended off, but smitten down.

— ALFRED THAYER MAHAN

Action is everything! The man who commits himself to continuous action in the vigorous pursuit of his goals has a tremendous advantage over the person who delays in the hope that something will turn up. As Napoleon said, "Opportunities? I *make* opportunities!"

The Battle for North Africa

In 1941, the Italian forces in North Africa had been badly beaten by the British. Mussolini appealed to Hitler to come to his aid. General Erwin Rommel, who later became a Field Mar-

37

shall, and the Deutsches Afrika Korps were sent to Tunisia to counter the British forces and retake the lost territory.

The British knew through their spies that a German expeditionary force was en route to Africa. They assumed, however, that they had ample time to prepare while the Germans unloaded their men and tanks and entrenched their forces. Because Rommel was a master of offensive warfare, as soon as the ship had docked and the men, tanks, trucks, and jeeps came off the boat, he launched them straight into battle, wave after wave.

The British were caught completely off guard. They reeled backward, desperately attempting to regroup and counterattack. But Rommel gave them no breathing room. He drove them all the way across North Africa to within sixty miles of Alexandria. He would have broken through and taken Egypt if he had had sufficient fuel and ammunition. The boldness and speed of Rommel's offensive against the British marked him as one of the finest combat generals of the twentieth century. The force that is on the offensive almost always has the advantage over the force that is defending or retreating.

The Strategy of the Offensive

Napoleon's armies won battle after battle, sweeping across Europe, using the principle of the offensive to continually attack, disperse, regroup, and attack once more. Often, when confronted with two armies, Napoleon would wheel and attack one of the armies before the second force could come up to its support. He would then turn and destroy the second force as well.

In the eighteenth century, Fredrick the Great united all of Prussia under a single king and doubled the area of his country with his innovations in warfare. His motto was, "L'audace, l'audace, et toujours l'audace"("Audacity, audacity, and always audacity").

His preferred strategy was to attack the enemy, whenever and wherever he found them. Although he lost many smaller battles, he won all the major contests and eventually became known as one of the greatest generals in European history.

"No great battles are ever won on the defensive."

—NAPOLEON

In Robert Green's book *The 48 Laws of Power*, he says, "When in doubt, act audaciously. Audacity will get you into trouble now and then, but even more audacity will usually get you out."

THE PRINCIPLE OF THE OFFENSIVE:
Seize, retain, and exploit the initiative.

The mark of the great commander, the excellent leader, the tremendously successful person is *courage*, and courage is always expressed in the willingness to go forward, to face danger, to take risks with no guarantee of success. All great success is achieved as the result of offensive action, doing something different, and usually faster and more forcefully than your competitor can react. Fortunately, courage is a virtue that can be developed by exercising and practicing it whenever it is required.

By maintaining the initiative, the commander preserves his freedom of action and enhances the morale of his troops. The principle of the offensive applies not only to offensive operations but also to the defensive. An offensive spirit must be inherent in the conduct of defensive operations, for prolonged and passive defense breeds unrest, lowers morale, and surrenders the advantage of intangibles to the enemy. An active defense, conducted with the spirit of the offensive, keeps the enemy off balance, restricts his ability to attack, and enhances security. In adhering to the principle of the offensive, the commander sets the pace and determines the course of battle, exploits enemy weaknesses, and is better prepared to capitalize on unexpected developments.

Seize the Day!

Courage is essential to success in all activities that call for risk and daring. As General Henri de Jomini said, "The most essential qualities of a general will always be: first, a high moral courage, capable of great resolution; second, a physical courage which takes no account of danger." Mark Twain wrote, "Courage is resistance to fear, mastery of fear—not absence of fear."

Winston Churchill wrote during World War II, "Courage is rightly considered the foremost of the virtues, for upon it, all others depend." If Darius had held firm at the Battle of Gaugamela instead of losing his nerve and fleeing, he might have used the overwhelming odds in his favor to defeat Alexander. Often, a hero is merely a coward who is brave five minutes longer.

Courage is a habit. You develop courage to face danger and risk by *acting* courageously. Ralph Waldo Emerson wrote that the most important lesson he learned as a young man was this:

"Make a habit throughout your life of doing the things you fear; if you do the thing you fear, the death of fear is certain."

The Principle of the Offensive Applied to Business

The goal of a business is to generate sales, revenues, and cash flow that are sufficient to assure the survival and growth of the enterprise. In business terms, a sales and marketing effort against entrenched competition is the equivalent of leading armies against entrenched enemy forces. In both cases, there is the possibility of success or failure, victory or defeat. In both cases, the commitment to the continuous offensive is essential for long-term success.

Business is not solely about making a profit. Business is about trying to *create and keep a customer*. When a business creates and keeps sufficient customers and provides them with products and services in a cost-effective manner, profits are the result. Offensive action in business, the creating and keeping of customers, supported by the artillery of advertising, marketing, public relations, promotional efforts, and sales activities, are the essential requirements for victory.

All strategic planning is therefore *customer* planning. All actions that take the offensive in the marketplace—in the sense of proactiveness and competing to win—are aimed at winning customers. The strategy of *excellent quality* in serving customers better than competitors do is the key to winning in tough markets.

Entrepreneurial Thinking

An entrepreneur is defined as someone who takes on the risk of a new business venture in the pursuit of profit. Entrepreneurship is inherently risky because there is no guarantee of success. Just as in taking offensive action in warfare, in business there is no guarantee of victory. Taking a chance on an entrepreneurial venture requires courage, daring, and a willingness to go forward in the face of potential loss.

Successful business people think entrepreneurially most of the time. Even in a large company, the ability to think like an entrepreneur in a fast-changing market is absolutely essential for survival and growth.

Entrepreneurs and business leaders have three special thinking qualities that make them different from the average person. These are: proactivity, responsibility, and result orientation.

Business leaders are *proactive* rather than reactive. They think, plan, and act decisively. They do not wait for things to happen—they make things happen. They seize the initiative whenever it is necessary, and they never stop until they achieve their goals.

This is quite different from the average person who tends to be *passive* in the face of adversity and rapid change. Most people are just waiting for someone to come along and tell them what to do and to help them out. They play it safe and never volunteer for anything. They are what Theodore Roosevelt called, "Those timid souls who know neither victory nor defeat."

The second quality of entrepreneurial thinking is that of *responsibility*. Entrepreneurs accept complete responsibility for themselves, for their companies, and for everything they do. Instead of making excuses, they make progress. They don't blame other people for their problems. They refuse to complain. They don't criticize or condemn. Instead, they say, "I am responsible!" They take charge, and get on with the job. George Washington said, "Ninety-nine percent of the failures come from people who have the habit of making excuses."

The top people in every field today view themselves as self-employed. They act as if they own the company they work for. They treat everything that happens in their organization as if it affected them personally. They are emotional, intense, and committed to the success of the business they work for. They believe in the concept of winning, of *victory*, and they are determined to help bring it about.

The third quality of leaders and entrepreneurs is that of *result orientation*. A continued focus on results keeps you moving forward. Result orientation forces you to continually set priorities and work on your highest value tasks. You continually ask, "What results are expected of me?" Whatever your answer to that question, minute-by-minute, hour-by-hour, that is what you should be working on all the time.

The most successful battle commanders are entrepreneurial in their thinking at all times. For example, during the Civil War, the Confederate stronghold at Vicksburg, Mississippi blocked Union control of the Mississippi River. General U.S. Grant first attacked the city by way of Chickasaw Bluffs and was repulsed. In 1863, Grant made four more unsuccessful attempts to capture or isolate Vicksburg. He kept trying new and different approaches. Finally, he managed to move his army across the Mississippi below Vicksburg, loop back North and attack Vicksburg from the East. After a series of marches and countermarches, including several small and large battles, in May Grant opened siege on Vicksburg and on July 4, 1863, the city fell, opening up the entire West to the Union forces. This battle arguably turned the course of the war. The most successful business leaders are entrepreneurial as well. Like courage, entrepreneurial ways of thinking and acting can be developed by continual practice.

Conduct Regular SWOT Analyses

Because you are *proactive, responsible,* and *result-oriented,* you are continually analyzing your current situation based on the realities of the moment, rather than on the way it might have been yesterday or the way it may be tomorrow.

The word SWOT is an acronym for *Strengths, Weaknesses, Opportunities,* and *Threats.* By continually evaluating your situation as if you were in enemy country, surrounded by hostile forces, you are better able to make the best decisions and to focus your energies where the best results are possible. The successful commander is one who can bring his greatest strengths to bear against the areas of greatest enemy weakness. At the beginning of World War II, the French felt secure behind the Maginot Line, the massive fortifications forming a zone ten to fifty miles deep that they had built along the country's eastern border between 1929 and 1934. The Germans' great advantage was speed and mobility. Using this strength to their advantage, they skirted the line and attacked through Belgium, which had refused to allow France to extend the Maginot Line along the Franco-Belgian border. From there, the Germans swept through the Ardennes Forest and across France, bringing about the unconditional surrender of the French Government in less than six weeks.

1. **Strengths.** What are your personal strengths? What are the strengths of your business? What are the strengths of the key people who report to you? What are the strengths of your products or services relative to your competition in today's marketplace? Be clear about your strengths, your areas of superiority, and always look for ways to capitalize on them.

2. **Weaknesses.** Where are you weak as a person? What are the weaknesses of your staff? What are the weaknesses of your products or services, based on feedback from your customers? What are the weaknesses in your current business situation, and what could you do to compensate for them? These are key questions you must ask and answer on a regular basis.

3. **Opportunities.** What opportunities are available to you to increase sales, cut costs, and improve your market position? What are the trends? Where is the market going? What is it that customers want today, and will want tomorrow, that you are not currently offering? Your greatest benefits and rewards will come from capitalizing on the opportunities of tomorrow rather than on being preoccupied with the problems of the past.

4. **Threats**. What are the threats to your business? What could possibly go wrong? What can you do to assure that you continue to survive and thrive no matter what happens? The failure to acknowledge and counter a possible threat can be disastrous to a company and to a military unit.

Conduct a SWOT analysis regularly on every part of your business, both internal and external. Make sure everyone around you is thinking in these terms as well. This keeps everyone sharp and alert and ready to act quickly when necessity demands it.

The Opportunities of Tomorrow

Whatever it is, it is already getting old. Within five years, 80 percent of all products and services offered today will be either obsolete or significantly modified from their current form. If a product works, it is already obsolete. Your competitors are bringing new products and services, and improvements on existing products and services, to the market faster than you can keep track. You can't afford to become complacent. You must be aggressively seeking out and developing the products and services that your customers will be demanding in the years ahead. If you don't, your competitors will. Your entire success will be determined by your ability to capitalize on the opportunities of today and tomorrow. What are they? Sometimes small innovations can lead to great victories, and even the downfall of empires. The invention of the longbow totally transformed warfare in the Middle Ages, allowing the peasants to defend themselves against the nobles. This led to an edict by Pope Innocent III in 1139 A.D. to ban the longbow as a danger to humanity. The stirrup, which gave an armed soldier or knight a firmer seat when fighting from horseback, was a critical invention that gave the forces of William of Normandy an advantage against the troops of the English king Harold II at the Battle of Hastings in 1066 and helped lead to the conquest of England.

In the modern age, laser guided bombs enable an attacking force to strike the enemy with such pinpoint accuracy that only small quantities of ordinance are required. This has changed the face of modern warfare and contributed to stunning victories in both Iraq in 1991, and Afghanistan in 2001–2002.

1. What *new* products and services could you develop and bring to the market? What *improvements* could you make to your existing products and services to make them better, faster, cheaper, and more desirable to your customers of today and your customers of tomorrow? Should you be getting into completely new product and service areas in order to better serve your customers? These are key questions that you must ask and answer continually.

2. What are the systems, processes, procedures, and activities within your company that could be improved, outsourced, downsized, or eliminated? Change is going to take place whether you like it or not. The only question is whether you will direct it or whether it will happen in a random and haphazard manner.

Continually look around you, seeking means of improving the way that you operate your business from the inside.

3. Strategic alliances: What are the different ways you could form alliances with people in businesses that are similar to your own and serve similar customers? A referral is worth fifteen cold calls on a new customer. How could you piggyback on the established credibility of other organizations to sell more of your product or service to the same type of customers?

4. Distribution channels: What additional opportunities exist for you to distribute more of your products or services through your existing distribution channels or through other distribution channels? Could you create new products and services that you could sell through new distribution channels that don't even exist for you today? What are all the different ways in which you could get more of your products and services to more of your customers in a profitable manner?

Don't Expect Perfection

You will have to try many different approaches in the course of your business career. According to the American Management Association, 70 percent of all managerial decisions will turn out to be wrong in the fullness of time. Two thirds of hires will turn out to be less than expected in the course of their employment. Virtually all successful people, including generals and military commanders, have made mistakes and failed in the past. The only one who has never failed is the person who has never tried very much. The key is to learn everything you can from every mistake. Then, put it behind you and try again. Be prepared to make mistakes. Be prepared to try lots of different things before you achieve a breakthrough of any kind.

George Washington lost almost every battle he fought during the Revolutionary War. The North lost every major engagement for the first three years of the Civil War. Winston Churchill was held responsible for the failure of the Gallipoli Campaign in World War I and again for the failure of the invasion of Norway in World War II. The Allies failed at Dieppe on August 19, 1942, in their first attempt to invade the Continent of Europe. But the lessons they learned served them well at the Battle of Normandy. The biggest successes in history have also been the biggest failures. But they were willing to face the possibility of failure in order to enjoy the rewards of success.

Innovate Continually

The most successful companies are those that continually innovate and develop new products and services both for existing markets and for new markets. Rubbermaid was famous for introducing one new product per day, year after year. The most successful high-tech companies are constantly introducing new products to the market, one after the other. Continuous innovation is a form of the continuous offensive. It keeps your competitors off balance and enables you to continue making powerful advances into the marketplace. The decision of General

George Washington to row his army across the river and attack the Hessian garrison at dawn on Christmas morning, catching them completely off guard and routing them, was an innovative act of military leadership that had a dramatic effect on the morale of the entire Colonial Army.

The Offensive Strategy of the Mongols

In 1220, three Mongol armies under Genghis Khan advanced along the Ferghana Valley to besiege Kojen, a major city of the Kwarazm Empire that consisted of part of present-day Iran, Turkmenistan, Uzbekistan, Tajikistan, and Afghanistan.

His generals Chagatai and Ogedei crossed the Irtysh River in the north and attacked Otrar where a group of Mongol envoys had been murdered three years before. The residents of the walled city barricaded themselves inside and resisted the Mongol attack. Thus began the "Mongol siege."

The Mongol siege was a continuous offensive, twenty-four hours a day, on a chosen section of the besieged city walls. Once it had begun, one third of the army attacked every eight hours, twenty-four hours a day, until the city fell. The sheer relentlessness of the Mongol siege was so devastating that no city ever withstood it. Every city that the Mongols besieged eventually fell and was subsequently destroyed along with all its inhabitants.

The principle of the continuous offensive is effective in warfare, business, politics, and personal life. The development and maintenance of forward motion increases confidence, courage, and energy in the attacker while ultimately fatiguing and demotivating the opposing forces. It also helps establish the reputation of the attacker as a force to be reckoned with.

The Marketing Offensive

There are five keys to offensive strategy in the marketplace. Each of these is essential. The failure to acknowledge or practice even one key marketing tactic can undermine or even eliminate your opportunities for success.

1. Specialization: What niche do you fill in the current market? What is your area of specialization? Do you specialize on the basis of a particular customer? Do you specialize on the basis of a particular need of a particular customer? Do you specialize in terms of serving a particular market?

When Harry Busch formed All-State Legal Supply, he decided to specialize in serving the needs of law firms, first in the East and then nationwide. Over the years he built a five-hundred-million-dollar company designed to satisfy a particular customer in a specialized customer niche. His entire focus was to create and make available more and more products and services in his area of specialization. What is yours?

The more specialized you are, the more effective your offense-related activities will be in getting and keeping customers. A major problem facing companies today is that they offer too many products and services at too many price points in too many markets. No one is exactly sure what they stand for or who their primary customer is supposed to be.

2. Differentiation. In what way is your product, service, or company different from and superior to that of your competitors?

Your ability to differentiate, to develop, and to maintain a *meaningful, competitive advantage* in a fast-changing marketplace is the key to your success and profitability.

What are you good at? For what part of your offerings do you receive the most positive compliments from your customers? If you were to do a market survey, what would your customers say that you do for them in an excellent fashion?

What is your competitive advantage *today*? What will it be in the *future* if you don't make any changes? What *should* it be if you want to dominate your market or another market? What *could* it be if you were to change your strategy and your positioning for the future? Your ability to differentiate your product from your competitors' in a meaningful way is the key to business growth and business advantage.

3. Segmentation: What are the specific market segments that you can dominate with your product or service offerings? Who are the specific or ideal customers in the marketplace who can most benefit from your competitive advantages? Your ability to accurately identify and segment your ideal customer market is the key to pinpoint focusing of your advertising and sales efforts.

Here is an exercise for you: Imagine preparing a newspaper advertisement for your ideal customers. How would you describe them? If you could select only one characteristic to define or identify an ideal customer, what would it be?

When you segment your market accurately, you can pinpoint your marketing, sales, advertising, and promotional activities and get more business at lower cost.

4. Concentration: This is your ability to concentrate single-mindedly on your very best potential customers, based on the first three tactics of marketing strategy. Who are they?

In the final analysis, your ability to *think* better than your competitors is your key strategic advantage. Your ability to plan, decide, and then take action to get more of the very best potential customers for what you sell is the highest form of business and entrepreneurial thinking. As Napoleon said, "The essence of strategy is, with the weaker army, always to have more force at the crucial point than the enemy." Focus all your energies and resources on convincing your ideal customer that what you offer is superior to anything offered by your competitors. This is the key to victory in business.

5. Positioning: In sales and marketing, perception is everything. How are you positioned in your marketplace? What do people think about you and what do they say about your company when you are not there? What are the words they use to describe you?

Your positioning very much affects your *brand image*. The position you hold in the hearts and minds of your customers and prospective customers determines whether they buy from you, how much they buy from you, how much they pay you for what you sell, how much they negotiate or delay making a sales purchase, and how often they both repurchase and refer you to other prospective customers. Your positioning is so important that you cannot leave it to chance.

The reason for the harshness of the Mongol siege described earlier was clear. It was a matter of positioning or "branding." Because news traveled fairly quickly over the caravan trails, it soon became known that it was much better to surrender to the Mongols than it was to resist them and suffer the consequences.

Genghis Khan made it clear that, if a city or even an empire surrendered to him, he would leave all of its administrators and tax collectors in place and allow them to live under a government of their own people as long as they paid proper tribute to the Mongols each year. This turned out to be a much better solution than going to war against them. It was one of the great marketing strategies of the Middle Ages.

The Principle of the Offensive in Your Personal Life

In order to take the offensive, you must first be courageous. Therefore the greatest obstacle to your success is the *fear of failure.* Actually, it is not failure that hurts you. You have failed lots of times in your life. It is the *fear* of failure that holds you back. Fear of any kind paralyzes you. It makes you step on the brake of your own potential. It undermines your confidence and diminishes your expectations of yourself.

The starting point for the development of courage is for you to set clear goals, make detailed plans, select the most important thing that you can do, and then dare to go forward!

Courage is the willingness to embark on a new course of action with no guarantees of success. In fact, you must expect to suffer temporary failure and defeat over and over again if you are really serious about being a big success. The fact is that successful people fail far more often than failures do. But the difference is that successful people expect to fail and expect to learn something valuable every time they fall down.

As long as you have a goal, when you do fall down, you will fall in a forward direction. When you pick yourself up, you will be a little closer to the goal each time. "There is no dishonor in falling, but only in failing to rise again."

The Corridor Principle

Dr. Robert Ronstadt taught entrepreneurship at Babson College in Massachusetts for several years. During this time, the college did a survey of the graduates of their M.B.A. Program in Entrepreneurial Studies. They found that less than 10 percent of the graduates of this program had actually started businesses and gone on to be successful entrepreneurs. What had happened?

Here is what they found. The major difference between the M.B.A. graduates of Babson College who succeeded and those who failed was that the successful people had had the courage to *launch*, to actually start a business and begin operations, while the others were still waiting. The successful entrepreneurs had received the same instruction as the unsuccessful entrepreneurs. But they summoned up their courage and stepped out in faith toward their goal of business success.

The other graduates, equally competent and well-educated, were still waiting for everything to be *just right*. Unfortunately, everything in life will never be just right. There will always be a hundred reasons why this is the wrong time to try anything new or different. The successful person is the person who takes action, who takes the offensive, even though the possibility for failure exists.

This is what they found: most of the people in the study achieved their success in a completely different area from what they had originally anticipated. No matter how good their business plans, no matter how carefully they started and operated, their great opportunities seemed to come from a different direction. They ended up succeeding with a different product or service, in a different field, selling to a different customer, who was buying the product or service for a different reason than they had expected when they started out.

When the successful entrepreneurs started toward their goals, it was as though they had entered a corridor toward a distant door where they thought their success would be. But as they moved through the corridor, obstacles and difficulties arose that blocked their passage. Simultaneously, to the right or left, new doors of opportunity opened up. Often, there were several of these unexpected diversions before they finally arrived at their goals of business success.

Buckminster Fuller called this the "Theory of Precession." He found that success almost always came from a different direction than anticipated. The key was the commitment to take action in the first place. Everything flowed from that. "Leap, and the net will appear!" This principle has been observed throughout the centuries in human affairs. It is absolutely essential for success. As you move forward on the offensive, you discover unexpected ways to achieve victory in ways you might not have seen or thought of if you played it safe.

You are like a guided missile. Because of the power of your subconscious and superconscious minds, once you have determined a goal, it is as if you have programmed a guidance mechanism in a sophisticated missile. You can then fire yourself off into life, and this guidance mechanism will direct you unerringly to your eventual target, even if you have no idea where it is when you start.

Once you know exactly what you want, you must have complete faith and trust that a series of universal powers is working to move you toward your goal and to move your goal toward you. This explains why "fortune favors the brave."

Never Stop Moving Forward

Confederate General Thomas J. "Stonewall" Jackson was one of the most formidable generals of the Civil War. His motto was to "mystify, mislead, and surprise." In his famous Shenandoah Valley Campaign, though greatly outnumbered by the Union armies, he was continually able to outmaneuver and defeat larger Union forces.

The secret of his success was that he was continually on the attack, shifting his infantry and cavalry to attack Union forces before they could combine against him. Because of the speed and effectiveness of his ongoing offensive actions, the Union Army greatly exaggerated his numbers and eventually pulled back out of the Shenandoah Valley to defend Washington.

Your brain contains a cybernetic mechanism that accepts continual feedback from your world and that allows you to self-correct as you move along. The more things you try, the more you *triumph*. The faster you move, the more experience you get. The more experience you get, the more competent you become. The more competent you become, the easier it is for you to make even better decisions in the future. You get faster and faster, and better and better, by staying in continuous motion toward your goal.

The faster you move, the more energy you have. The faster you move, the more alert you are. The faster you move, the happier you feel. The faster you move, the greater sense of control you experience. The faster you move, the more you get done and the more opportunities there are that open up for you.

The Principle of the Offensive Revisited

All successful people, military commanders, entrepreneurs, business people, salespeople, and self-responsible individuals practice the principle of the continuous offensive as they move toward their goals and objectives. Once you get going, keep going. When you incorporate the principle of the offensive into your business and personal life, and you refuse to stop, you eventually become unstoppable.

CHAPTER THREE

The Principle of the Mass

Concentrate
Your Powers

When you have resolved to fight a battle, collect your forces. Dispense with nothing. A single battalion sometimes decides the day.   —NAPOLEON

The ability to focus and concentrate is essential for success in any competitive endeavor. Great commanders and business leaders are those who are most capable of bringing all their resources to bear on the actions or goals that are critical for success.

The Battle of Isandhlwana

The British Expeditionary Force of 2,600 men under Lord Chelmsford advanced into Zululand in January 1879 with banners flying, completely confident in their ability to defeat the armies of the Zulu Chief, King Cetewayo. After three days of marching, the army stopped at a rocky outcrop named

Isandhlwana to rest. Violating one of the first principles of warfare, "Never divide your forces in the face of the enemy," Lord Chelmsford took 1,600 men with him on a day's march from the main camp in response to a report of an encounter by British troops with a large Zulu force.

Zulu spies had been watching the British army from the hills and relaying their observations back to the rest of the Zulu army. With the British army divided, the Zulu warriors saw their chance and took it.

Even though they had been warned by their Natal scouts about the formidable fighting power of the Zulu army, the British troops at Isandhlwana had dispersed over a large area and become casual about their defenses.

Suddenly the Zulus attacked, using their "Buffalo Head" formation. In the Buffalo attack strategy, the Zulu army was divided into four sections. The first section, the *head* of the Buffalo, attacked the British soldiers frontally, throwing them back. The second and third sections, the *horns*, swarmed out on either flank to envelop the enemy. The fourth group, the *loins*, was held in reserve.

The British force of 1,800 men at Isandhlwana was quickly overwhelmed and wiped out. Only 55 men survived. They had dispersed their forces, spreading them over a wide area, completely giving up their ability to concentrate and counter the attack of the Zulus. It was the worst defeat ever inflicted on an army of the British Empire by native forces.

The Battle of Rorke's Drift

The Zulu army, several thousand strong, and emboldened by its victory at the battle of Isandhlwana, immediately set out under the leadership of the king's brother to wipe out the combination mission station and trading post at Rorke's Drift across the border in Natal, less than one day's march away. The Battle of Rorke's Drift lasted two days. The 140 enlisted men and officers held off wave after wave of attack by more than 4,000 Zulu warriors. At the end of the battle, the Zulus retreated back into their homeland. They never again won a major battle against a British force.

What was the difference between these two battles, which took place in the same week? The soldiers at Rorke's Drift were able to mass together and concentrate their fire throughout the two-day battle. They were able to consolidate their defense of the mission station with a tight perimeter. The much larger British force at Isandhlwana was dispersed over a wide area. They went into battle piecemeal, unable to concentrate their forces or their fire. In the battle of Isandhlwana, the disciplined Zulu regiments, called impis, massed their attack and destroyed the British forces. Even though the Zulus were armed only with light spears and shields, they were able to defeat the better armed British forces using the power of concentration.

THE PRINCIPLE OF THE MASS:
Concentrate combat power at the decisive place and time.

The commander must choose the proper time and place. Determining the right time and place requires a combination of judgment, timing, good military intelligence, and all the factors that go into creating and deploying an effective combat force. The right time and place is highly fluid, ever-changing in the "Fog of War." The commander must also determine what combat power is available to him and how much is needed. Since combat power is the total of physical means and moral means available to a commander, his available combat power is a function of numbers, quality, and state of morale. The principle of the mass leads to success when a commander achieves superiority in combat power over his rival. Through proper application of the principle of the mass, numerically superior forces can be defeated.

The Principle of the Mass Applied to Business

Sales and profitability are twin essentials for business success. Your ability to concentrate your limited resources and energies on your greatest potential opportunities for sales and profitability is key to your success.

A business usually begins with a single product or service for which it sees a need that is not currently being satisfied in the market. Often, the entrepreneur believes that he can offer a product or service that is superior to the competition. In each case, the ability to concentrate single-mindedly on producing and vigorously selling a superior product is essential for victory.

The opposite of concentration is *diffusion of effort*—a tendency to offer too many products and services to too many types of customers, in too many ways, with too many different price points. This inevitably leads to loss of energy, overextension, excessive costs, and the diversion of key talents away from the areas where great success is possible.

The Citadel Strategy

In the days of walled cities, a city was often built with concentric walls, like the rings of a target, from the outside to the inside. If the enemy breached the first wall, the defenders retreated to the second wall. If that wall was breached, the defenders retreated inward to the third wall. The highest and most defensible part of the city was called the redoubt, or the *citadel*.

The citadel represented the last stronghold of defense. When all was lost, the king and his family, the key people in the city, and the royal guard withdrew to the citadel where they attempted to hold out until they were rescued by a neighboring power.

What is the citadel in your business? If the sales of your products and services dropped dramatically, on what few products or services would you concentrate and focus all of your efforts in order to survive? Whatever your answer, this is your *core* business. This is the most important product or service you offer. This is where you must continually mass and concentrate your forces to achieve and maintain sales and profitability.

Your core business is made up of those products or services that you produce and deliver in an *excellent* fashion. These are the products or services that your customers like above all others. These are also your most profitable products and services. They represent the essence of what you do, and they are the major reasons for your profitability and growth up to now.

In Chris Zook and James Allen's book *Profit from the Core*, they show that businesses succeed when they concentrate on their core, and they fail when they get too far from their core. If, for any reason, your business is not as profitable as you would like it to be, the solution is usually to get back to doing what you do best and most profitably. Get back to your core.

Gary Hamel and C. K. Prahalad, in their book *Competing for the Future*, emphasize that the key to strategic success, both in the present and in the future, is to identify your core competencies and then focus on getting better and better in those key areas. Your core competencies are the special skills and abilities that enable you and your company to produce excellent products and services and even to dominate your market. Your core competencies are the foundation of all business success. No business success is possible without essential core competencies developed and deployed at a high level. What are yours?

Concentrating Your Powers for Business Success

As your market changes, you should regularly take time out to identify your most profitable products and services. What are they today? What are they likely to be tomorrow? What could they be? What should they be? Of all the products and services that you offer, if you had to retreat to your citadel, what one or two products and services would you continue to produce and sell?

Who are your most important customers? Who are the people who buy from you the most readily, and from whom you earn the highest profits? Who are the 20 percent of your customers that account for 80 percent of your sales revenues? What is your plan to keep these customers and to create more of them?

Who are your most important people internally? Who are the people in your business whom you depend upon the most for the success of your enterprise? Who are the 20 percent of your staff, either internally or externally, who produce 80 percent of the results that your company depends on? Develop a plan to retain, appreciate, and reward your key people before someone comes along and hires them away.

What are your most successful methods of marketing and sales? Which are the most effective? On a cost per sale basis, where do you get the biggest *bang for your buck* in sales and marketing expenditures? Based on this analysis, what should you be doing more of—or less of—in sales and marketing?

Many companies dramatically increase their revenues by reorienting their marketing efforts and *focusing* on a specific market segment to the exclusion of all others. Would this make sense for you?

The Battle of Austerlitz

Napoleon achieved one of his greatest victories at the battle of Austerlitz in Moravia on December 2, 1805, by using the principle of the mass. The combined forces of Alexander I of Russia and Francis I of Austria outnumbered him, and they were well positioned on the battlefield. Nonetheless, he defeated them by concentrating all of his forces on seizing the Pratzen Heights, the high point in the center of the battlefield, which was occupied by the Russians. If he could control the highest point in the battlefield, he could move his reserves and mask his attacks against the Austrian and Russian Armies.

When the battle began, Napoleon had 73,000 men and 139 guns. The combined forces of the Austrians and the Russians were 85,500 men and 278 guns. The battle raged back and forth from 7:00 in the morning until about 2:00 in the afternoon, but the French were eventually victorious. By concentrating all of their forces on the key objective, they were able to seize the commanding heights of the battlefield and dominate the fight.

From this point, Napoleon was able to operate from the Pratzen Heights lashing out against the allied columns on his south and north. Napoleon's genius was in continually shifting his forces so that he had superior numbers at each point of attack. By 4:30 P.M., the battle was over. The Austro/Russian casualties amounted to more than 27,000 men. The French lost only 8,300. This was one of the decisive battles in European history. It was a classic application of the principle of the mass.

Just as Alexander the Great concentrated his forces and led his elite companion cavalry in a focused attack on the enemy center at the Battles of Issus and Arbela, great generals win battles by concentrating and massing superior strength at the right time and the right place to assure victory. Selecting the right time and place to concentrate your powers is always a matter of judgment based on many factors. Selecting the right time and place comes from training, experience, good intelligence, and luck.

Key Result Areas

Identify the key result areas of your business. What are the *results* that your company, and your products or services, absolutely have to get to satisfy your customers?

Identify the key result areas of each person on your staff, including yourself. What do *you* absolutely, positively have to do in an excellent fashion to get the results that are expected of you? Once you have identified your personal key result areas, you must then set *standards of performance* in each area. How do you measure those results?

A key result area has three qualities: First, it is clear, specific, and measurable. Second, it is the sole responsibility of a single person; if that person does not do it, it will not be done by someone else. Third, a key result is an output of the job that becomes an input for the job of someone else.

A key result area may be *closing a sale*. This result is specific and measurable. It is the responsibility of a particular salesperson. The sales order then becomes an *input* to the people who have to process the sale, produce the product or service, deliver or install it, bill for it, and service it afterwards.

In management, the innovation and development of new products and services is a key result area. It is something that must be done. It is measurable. It is usually under the authority of, or the responsibility of, a single person. Once it is complete, it becomes an input to the manufacturing, marketing, sales, and delivery functions of the business.

These are called "key result areas" because, if they are not done, and done well, in a timely fashion, they can lead to failure in a job or even in an entire company.

For example, a key result area is *leadership*. If a company does not have competent and committed leaders who are capable of making the right decisions and getting the job done in a timely fashion, the company will eventually go out of business.

Because key result areas are measurable, you can attach a standard of performance to each one. Even better, you can attach a standard of *excellent* performance to each one. How a person accomplishes his key result areas and the standards of performance he reaches becomes the basis for all rewards and promotion within the organization.

With key result areas and standards of performance, people know exactly what they are expected to do, and to what standard, and what rewards or consequences go along with successful performance. Ideally, everyone should know the key result areas and standards of performance of each coworker, and even the boss. This is the key to effective teamwork and concentrated effort.

Critical Success Factors

In every business, and in every part of the business, there are a few critical success factors or benchmarks that you can use to measure performance and results in each part of the organization at any time.

These measures can be as simple as daily sales volume, or they can be as complex as gross sales revenue per person employed in the company. One of the most important things you can do to help you concentrate your attention is to select the few critical success factors or measures that can most quickly and accurately give you a reading on the key parts of your business.

When I was developing real estate, I built a pizza restaurant in one of my shopping centers. The owner, a successful entrepreneur named Peter, had several restaurants in different parts of the city. Each time a pizza order was taken, it was written up on a sales slip that was put on a spike on top of the cash register. This was Peter's critical success measure. He could walk into any restaurant, at any time of day and, by looking at the number of sales slips on the spike, he would have an immediate idea of how well the restaurant was doing that day.

What numbers go onto your spike? Most businesses focus on daily, weekly, and monthly sales. Many individuals focus on the amount they earn per week, month, or year. Successful entrepreneurs think in terms of how much they earn each day. The most successful people think in terms of how much they earn each *hour*. This becomes their benchmark for personal performance and financial results.

Your ability to select the correct *critical success factors*, and then to concentrate on improving those numbers, is a key responsibility of leadership. If the numbers you choose are the right ones for your business, a single number can reveal a lot about what is going on throughout the enterprise.

The Profit Model

Most companies sell a variety of products and services. The danger in being a "mini-conglomerate" is that you can very easily lose track of the exact costs of producing a product or service and selling it in a competitive market. It may happen that many of the products or services that you are selling today are not really yielding you the kind of profit you *think* they are. In fact, you could be losing money on your best-selling items and not even know it. Many companies think they know which product is their best-seller and consequently which product they should concentrate the bulk of their resources behind. Before you make any assumptions, however, you need to make sure you are making a profit on that product and that you are using your resources effectively.

One of the most important decisions you can make is to isolate each product or service you sell and then *accurately* determine all the costs involved in the production and sale of that product. Allocate a portion of the rent, the staff and administrative costs, the utilities and telephone bills, the advertising and promotion, and a part of every variable cost that you can identify.

Determine exactly how many hours of executive time it takes to sell and deliver this product. How many returns do you receive? What is your average gross and net profit per sale? When you itemize every single cost attached to a product or service, you will often find out that some of your best-selling products or services are not yielding you very much profit at all. In fact, many companies find out that they are selling a product or service at a loss and at *high* volume.

If you have an entrepreneurial mentality, you are probably not very interested in the accounting and bookkeeping functions necessary to determine the exact costs or expenses associated with a particular product or service. In that case, hire an accountant, give her the necessary instructions with regard to allocating direct costs, indirect costs, fixed costs, variable costs, and semi-variable costs to your top 20 percent of products or services. Have her break out the costs and revenues of each product down to the penny.

You may find that a product that you have been taking for granted is your biggest moneymaker. Meanwhile, a product that you have been selling in large quantities hardly makes you any profit at all. Whatever the case may be, it is important that you find out for yourself so that you can concentrate your energies and resources on selling more of the products and services that yield you the highest net profits from everything you do.

The Principle of the Mass Applied to Personal Success

The key to personal success is for you to do more and more of those things that you enjoy the most, and get paid the most for doing, and simultaneously, for you to do fewer and fewer of those things that you don't like and which don't pay you very much.

In Chapter 1, The Principle of the Objective, I explained the importance of setting goals and gave you a seven-step method that you can use to set and achieve any goal you want for the rest of your life. I also mentioned the central importance of your *major definite purpose*. This is the one goal, the attainment of which will have the greatest positive impact on your life. You should know what this goal is and be working on it every single day.

Be Clear About Your Goals

The principle of the mass has perhaps the greatest impact of all when it is applied to your goals. Your ability to decide exactly what you want and then to concentrate all your energies on achieving your most important goals probably determines your success and happiness more than any other decision you make.

Decide how much money you want to earn each month and each year. Write it down. Make a plan. Work on your plan every day.

Set goals for the amount of money that you want to accumulate sometime in the future, and focus on achieving this amount every month. Leave nothing to chance.

Decide what you want for your family and in your relationships with the important people in your life. Write these goals down, and do something to attain them each day.

Set goals for how healthy and fit you want to be. Create diet and exercise plans that you work on every day to help you live a long, happy life.

When you focus and concentrate on clear, written, measurable goals, combined with time lines and action plans, you accomplish vastly more than the average person who simply acts and reacts to whatever is going on around him.

Develop the Skills You Require

Just as a company requires core competencies to survive and thrive, both in the present and in the future, so do you. Identify your special talents and skills. What are your natural abilities and interests? What is it that you are good at? Even more important, what is it that you *could* be good at if you set it as a goal, made a plan, and worked on it every day?

Knowledge and know-how are the keys to success in the twenty-first century, and your skill set is becoming obsolete with every passing year. Whatever got you to where you are today is not enough to keep you there. You must be continually thinking forward, into the future, and identifying the skills you will need to be able to make an excellent living in the years ahead.

Ask this question regularly: "What one skill, if I developed and did it in an excellent fashion, would have the greatest positive impact on my career?"

Whatever your answer to that question, make a plan to acquire that skill or to improve in that area. If you are not sure what that key skill might be, ask your boss. Ask your co-workers. If necessary, take tests to measure your level of competence in the important parts of your job. Your ability to ask and answer this question correctly will largely determine how much you earn and accomplish in the years ahead.

Do Something Every Day

Every great success is an accumulation of many small efforts and actions that no one ever sees or appreciates. It is the little things you do each day, every day, that eventually add up to a great life.

Decide on the daily actions that can help you the most. Resolve to focus and concentrate on those key actions as a part of your regular work routine. When in doubt, always think in terms of the specific things that you can do right now.

The more action-oriented you become, the greater sense of control you experience. The more you feel in control of yourself and your life, the happier and more effective you will be. Action is everything.

The Principle of the Mass Applied to Time Management

The primary reason that people succeed in life is because they identify the most important task they can accomplish, at any given time, and then focus single mindedly on completing that task before anything else. This is the entirety of time management. All time management systems are developed to help you identify that critical task and get you going on it before you do anything else of lower value.

In my book *Eat That Frog!* I give twenty-one key ideas that you can use to set priorities, overcome procrastination, and get the job done fast. The most important principle of the book is the significance of starting on your most important task immediately, and then disciplining yourself to concentrate on that single task until it is 100 percent complete. When you can do that, you will have conquered yourself. You can then go on to achieve any goal you set for yourself.

The Productivity Curve

Imagine a curve that slopes down from a high point on the left to a low point on the right. This is your "Productivity Curve." At the high end of the curve, the things you do have great value. At the low end of the curve, the things you do have little or no value at all.

Where you choose to work on your own productivity curve largely determines what you will accomplish in your work and personal life. Successful people discipline themselves to work at the top of the curve most of the time. Unsuccessful people unwittingly allow themselves to slide down the curve. They spend the day working at things that are not particularly important or valuable.

Here is the key point. Whatever you do *repeatedly* becomes a new habit. You either develop the habit of working at the top of your curve, doing things that really make a difference to yourself and your company, or by *default* you will end up working at the bottom of your curve, doing things that really don't matter at all. The choice is yours. And you make this choice every time you select a particular task to work on.

The Pareto Principle

Perhaps the most famous time management principle of all is the *Pareto Principle*, first developed by the Italian economist Vilfredo Pareto in 1895. After years of research, he concluded that society could be divided into two groups, the "vital few," the top 20 percent who controlled most of the money, and the "trivial many," the bottom 80 percent who owned very little.

He concluded, and proved mathematically, that the top 20 percent of people in any society ended up owning 80 percent of the wealth. Further studies with the Pareto Principle have shown that this ratio applies to almost any economic activity. For example, 20 percent of your customers will purchase 80 percent of your products or services. Of all the things you sell, 20 percent contribute 80 percent of the profits. On your staff, 20 percent of your people will produce 80 percent of the results that your company achieves.

In time management, the Pareto Principle says that 20 percent of the things you do will account for 80 percent of the value of all the things you do. The key to high productivity is for you to identify your top 20 percent of tasks and activities before you begin. It is then crucial to work on those "vital few" single-mindedly all day long. You must simultaneously avoid getting distracted by the bottom 80 percent of tasks that contribute very little value to your life or work.

The Principle of Three

Here is an exercise: make a list of everything you do at work. Ask yourself, "If I could only do *one* thing on this list, which one task contributes the greatest value to my company?"

Once you have identified the most valuable thing you do, ask yourself, "What is the second most valuable thing I do? What is the third?"

In most jobs, there seem to be *three* critical tasks that you perform that contribute most of the value of the work you do. Of these three, one task will usually be more important than the other two, and the other two are more important than any of your other tasks. Your job is to identify these three tasks, in order of priority, and then to work exclusively in these areas until every task is 100 percent complete. This is the key to excellent time management.

Consider the Consequences

The easiest way to set priorities on your time and your work is to ask the question: "What are the potential *consequences* of doing or not doing this task?" An important task or activity has significant potential consequences. An unimportant task has low or *no* potential consequences.

By "potential consequences" I mean that if you perform this task excellently, and in a timely fashion, it can have a major impact on your career and your future. And all your tasks can be ranked in an order or priority from the task having the greatest possible consequences to the task having the least number of consequences.

Imagine that you were to be called out of town unexpectedly for a month. Of all your current tasks, which one task would you want to get finished before you left? *This* is your top priority. This will almost invariably be the one task that has the greatest potential consequences for successful completion.

Ask yourself, "If I could only do one thing all day long, which one task contributes the greatest value to my company or my income?" This is another question to help you identify and focus on your highest priority at work.

Ask yourself, "What can I, and only I, do, that if done well, can make a real difference to my company?" There is only one answer to this question at any one given time. Your ability to ask and answer this question and then to do this one thing is a key to high levels of personal productivity and effectiveness.

What Is Holding You Back?

The theory of constraints, popularized by Elihu Goldratt in his book *The Goal*, says that, in any work process, there is a limiting step or constraint that determines the speed at which the entire process can be completed. To get more done, you must identify the key constraints on your activities. You do this by asking these two questions: 1) What is my goal or objective? and 2) Why haven't I accomplished this goal or objective *already*?

In other words, what is holding you back? What sets the *speed* at which you achieve your most important goal? Is your constraint *internal* either to yourself or to your company? Is your constraint *external*, caused or created by forces outside yourself or your organization?

Your ability to identify the critical constraint that determines the speed at which you achieve your most important goal is essential to your getting the job done in a timely fashion.

Once you have identified your key constraint, you must then focus and concentrate all of your energies on alleviating that constraint or solving that problem. Sometimes the removal of one key constraint can alter the entire situation. The hiring of one key person, or the acquisition of one key skill or resource, can totally change the future of your business.

Often, you are only one key skill or ability away from doubling your income, and dramatically increasing your productivity and effectiveness. What could it be?

Practice Single Handling in All Things

The principle of the mass applies to every area of business and personal life. Your ability to identify the most important thing you can do and then to "single handle," to concentrate without diversion or distraction on that one task or activity, is the key to high productivity. For example, the Marines are famous for focusing single-mindedly on achieving their objective. The inability to concentrate leads to wasted time, wasted energy, diffusion of effort, poor performance, underachievement, frustration, and eventual failure.

Peter Drucker says, "Whenever you find something getting done, you find a *monomaniac* with a mission." Successful people all seem to have this special ability to concentrate their forces and mass their energies on the critical task where great success and victory is possible.

Fortunately, focus and concentration are habits and ways of acting that you can learn with practice. Once you have developed the ability to set priorities and concentrate single-mindedly on the most valuable use of your time, your future becomes unlimited.

The Principle of the Mass Revisited

Great men and women and leaders in every area of life are those who have learned to focus on their critical tasks. In warfare, the ability to mass your forces at the right time and place is a force multiplier that enables smaller forces to conquer a larger enemy. An average person with average abilities and opportunities can often achieve outstanding success by concentrating on doing one thing, the most important thing, and doing it well.

There are many qualities that are helpful in achieving success, but the qualities of focus and concentration are *indispensable*. With the ability to mass your powers, all things are possible. You become unstoppable and your ultimate victory is virtually guaranteed.

The Principle of Maneuver

Remain Flexible at All Times

One does not plan and then try to make circumstances fit those plans. One tries to make plans fit the circumstances. I think the difference between success and failure in high command depends upon the ability, or lack of it, to do just that.

—GENERAL GEORGE S. PATTON

Almost all great military victories are battles of movement, maneuver, and unexpected swift action by one side to gain the advantage over the opposing force.

Most failures in battle are the result either of being outmaneuvered by the opposing force or of the failure on the part of the commanding general to adapt and respond appropriately to changes in the immediate situation. The principle of maneuver explains much of the success and failure in personal and business life as well.

The Palatinate Campaign

General George Patton used the single and double envelopment principle of maneuver with perhaps the greatest frequency and effectiveness in military history. His stated philosophy was, "Grab 'em by the nose and kick 'em in the ass!"

His attack strategy was to launch his infantry forward in a frontal assault on the German positions. The German forces responded by moving their reserves forward to meet the attack. Patton then swung his armored columns around the enemy's right or left flank, or both, and cut them off from behind.

In his 1945 Palatinate Campaign in Germany, he used this single and double envelopment strategy repeatedly, eventually encircling, cutting off, and capturing more than 350,000 German soldiers with very few casualties to his own forces.

THE PRINCIPLE OF MANEUVER:
Move and position military forces in a way that
furthers the accomplishment of the mission.

Maneuver is also a corollary of the principle of the mass, for it is another means of achieving a decisive superiority of combat power. Movement and positioning must always be undertaken with the intent to place the enemy at a relative disadvantage. Proper movement and positioning frequently achieve results that otherwise could be achieved only at heavy cost in men and matériel. In many situations, the principle of maneuver can be applied only in conjunction with the effective employment of firepower.

The Principle of Maneuver in Business

Whatever got you to where you are today is not enough to keep you there. Your products, services, processes, sales, advertising, and marketing strategies and tactics are all becoming obsolete at a rapid rate. Your ability to continually come up with faster, better, newer, and more original ways to conduct your business and sell your products or services is absolutely vital to your success in a fast-changing, turbulent marketplace.

In their book *Military Misfortunes: The Anatomy of Failure in War* the authors Eliot A. Cohen and John Gooch identify three reasons for failure in warfare. These three reasons apply to business as well. They are failure to anticipate, failure to learn, and failure to adapt.

The first, *failure to anticipate*, refers to the inability or unwillingness of the commander to look down the road into the future and think about all of the possible actions that a competitor could take to defeat your forces.

At the beginning of the personal computer age, Apple Computer came to the market with the strategy of "firstest with the mostest," which was used with devastating effectiveness by Confederate General Nathan Bedford Forrest during the Civil War. Apple developed a computer with a friendly name that was easy to set up and easy to use. It was an amazing market success.

Apple was followed by other companies with similar products, especially the personal computer from IBM with its MS-DOS operating system, developed for them by a small company out of Bellevue, Washington, named Microsoft.

Both Steve Jobs and Bill Gates, the commanders of their corporate armies, looked down the road into the future of personal computing, operating systems, and software. Steve Jobs made the strategic decision to protect Apple's operating system and software within a closed system. In so doing, he could charge higher prices and earn fully 50 percent profit on sales. As long as Apple Computer was the favorite choice of so many people, customers were willing to pay premium prices and give Apple Computers premium profits.

General Bill Gates looked down the road into the future of personal computers and saw a different picture. His goal was "a personal computer for every person, on every desk." He concluded that the more different programs that could be developed to run on the same operating system, the more manufacturers would want to install that operating system on their computers at the factory.

He therefore made the Microsoft Operating System available to software designers worldwide. His strategy turned out to be right. Today, Microsoft Windows 95, 98, 2000, and XP are installed in 90 percent of new computers and used worldwide by virtually everyone. Apple, by attempting to safeguard its high profit margins, now controls less than 5 percent of the market. Bill Gates anticipated correctly. Steve Jobs did not. The difference in market terms has been extraordinary.

Failure to learn from mistakes is another reason for business and military defeat. Thomas J. Watson, Jr., longtime chairman of IBM, once said, "We don't mind if people make mistakes around here. This is normal and natural. What is unforgivable is the failure to learn from the mistakes, which leads to repeating them."

Whenever something goes wrong in your business, treat it as a learning experience. Extract every bit of wisdom that you can from the mistake or setback. Imagine that the failure or problem has been sent to teach you something that you need to know to be more successful in the future. When you extract every kernel of knowledge and wisdom from every mistake, you learn and grow at a rapid rate.

The third reason for military and business misfortune is the *failure to adapt*. This is where the principle of maneuver is so important. No matter how carefully you have thought through your goals, objectives, and plans, remember the adage, "No strategy ever survives first contact with the enemy."

Be prepared to accept feedback and self-correct quickly. Resolve to adapt, adjust, and respond in an effective manner when the situation changes. Do not allow yourself to fall in love with a particular product, service, or way of doing business. Always be open to the possibility that you could be wrong.

Zero-Based Thinking

The management guru Peter Drucker always recommends that you examine every part of your business regularly to determine if there is anything that you are doing that you wouldn't get into again today if you had it to do over. I call this the process of "zero-based thinking." It is one of the most important thinking tools you can use to remain fluid and flexible in a fast-changing environment.

Apply the following question to every part of your business: "Is there anything that I am doing today that, knowing what I now know, I wouldn't get into again today if I had to do it over?"

This is what I call a "KWYNK Analysis." KWYNK stands for "Knowing What You Now Know." Asking and answering this question of everything you do can save or gain you enormous amounts of time and money.

Start with your products or services. Is there any product or service that you are offering that, knowing what you now know, you wouldn't bring to the marketplace?

Investments in managerial ego are often the main obstacle to discontinuing a product or service that is obviously unsuccessful. This happens because people become confused over the difference between *variable costs* and *sunk costs*. People become determined to recoup the costs of bringing a product to the market because they don't realize that those are sunk costs.

A sunk cost is an amount that you have spent that is irretrievable. It is gone forever. You can never get it back. If the sunk cost has yielded a profitable product or service as the result of research, development, production, sales, and marketing, you are fortunate. You must face the fact that most products eventually fail, no matter how much intelligence and research has gone into developing them in the first place.

Be willing to admit that your business is full of sunk costs. Be willing to "cut your losses" if you are currently promoting a product or service that the market does not particularly want or is not willing to pay for. Focus on the product and service opportunities of tomorrow rather than on the problem products or services of yesterday. Focus on the products and services that yield the very highest profits, and commit more of your resources to selling more of these products or services into your current market before it changes.

The Battle of Waterloo

At 6:00 P.M. on June 18, 1815, the Duke of Wellington was losing the Battle of Waterloo. He turned to the officers around him and said, "Give me Blücher or give me night." He was referring to the anticipated arrival of the Prussian army under General Blücher, without which the advancing French forces would soon overwhelm him.

At this critical moment, the French General Ney urged Napoleon to order his Imperial Guard, a crack veteran force of 10,000 troops, into the final attack. But Napoleon felt that the battle was won and refused to commit his final reserves. At that moment, General Blücher and the 50,000 men of the Prussian army emerged from the woods and attacked the French right flank, causing it to reel backward and begin to roll up like a carpet.

At 6:30 P.M., Napoleon realized his mistake. He quickly reversed his division and ordered his Imperial Guard to go forward. But it was too late. The defeat of the French had already begun. The British troops under Wellington, excited and exhilarated by the appearance of Blücher, counterattacked all along the line.

The French forces, who had been on the verge of victory just minutes before, were pushed back. When the Imperial Guard finally went forward, it was beaten back and forced to retreat for the first time in its history. The French were soon overwhelmed and surrounded by the onrushing British forces. By 7:00 P.M., the battle became a rout. The French army was scattered, chased, and hunted down across the countryside. They lost more than 50,000 men. The age of Napoleon was over. He died in exile on St. Helena a few years later.

Many companies make similar mistakes. They spend their time, money, energy, and valuable resources promoting products or services that the market does not want or that are not superior to others offered by competitors. Meanwhile, their very best products and services languish on the shelves without sufficient money or energy behind them to maximize their possibilities and profits. Don't let this happen to you.

Continually Evaluate Every Person

Apply the KWYNK formula to every person who works with you and every company that you do business with on the outside. "Is there anyone who, *knowing what you now know*, you would not hire, assign, enter into an agreement with, or even acquire as a customer?"

According to the Pareto Principle, discussed in Chapter 3, 20 percent of your people do 80 percent of the work. This means that 80 percent of your people are only doing 20 percent of the work and are usually receiving full pay. Fully one third of the people you hire will not work out over time. Is there anyone working for or with you today that you would not hire again today if you had it to do over?

One of the kindest things that you can do is to let a person go if they have no long-term future with your company. It is heartless and cruel to keep a person in a job if, in your heart, you know that this person is not going to work out in the long term. Have the courage and confidence to cut your losses, pull the plug, and set the person free.

Look Inside Your Company

Is there anything that you are doing inside your company that, knowing what you now know, you wouldn't start up again if you had to do it over? Is there any commitment of people, resources, money, or time that you have made that is not yielding the results that you expected? According to the American Management Association, 70 percent of your decisions will turn out to be wrong over time. Many of the things that you are doing today are things that you would not get into again today if you had to do them over again. What are they?

Is there any commitment of advertising, promotion, sales, or other dollars that you would not make again today, knowing what you now know, based on the results that you have gotten from these investments or expenditures? Jim Collins, in his book *From Good to Great*, says that great companies and great executives are those who are willing to ask themselves the "brutal questions" about their businesses. You should be prepared to ask yourself, and others, the brutal questions about anything that you are doing and any expenditure that you are currently making. Some of the answers that you get back may surprise you.

The "knowing what you now know" question, continually applied to every aspect of your business, keeps you honest, alert, and prepared to *anticipate, learn, and adjust* in the face of fast-changing circumstances. Your ability to ask and answer this question accurately is the mark of the superior thinker and the business genius. It can be the key to victory.

The American Revolution

The generalship of George Washington has been both praised and criticized for more than 200 years. He never really won a major battle until the siege of Yorktown and yet he defeated the British and won the Revolutionary War for the United States. How is this possible?

When the war with Britain began, George Washington and the other Colonial officers who enlisted were all men with experience in the British army of the day. They had often fought against the Indians and the French in the years prior to the Declaration of Independence. Their schooling in military affairs was largely that of Continental warfare, which involved large masses of armed men maneuvering on open ground in set-piece battles.

The recruits to the Colonial army were completely different from the regulars in the British army. They were independent farmers, craftsmen, merchants, and landowners. They were highly individualistic, a typically American trait that runs through the American character even today. They had neither the training, the discipline, nor the willingness to line up in mass formations and march against an enemy that was usually vastly superior in experience and firepower and that was massed against them.

After the Colonists had been defeated in several battles and skirmishes, George Washington decided to change the rules of battle in America. He invented an entirely new strategy of warfare, what is called today "guerilla warfare." He had the rare ability to adjust his plans to actual circumstances, and to find a way to achieve the main aim of ultimate victory by alternate means.

This bold action by Washington—changing the ways and means of conducting a war while in the very middle of a war— was the critical factor that determined the success of the Thirteen Colonies in the Revolutionary War.

By resorting to *hit-and-run* guerilla tactics, Washington was able to use the principle of maneuver to great advantage. While the British continually pressed for a decisive engagement that would conclusively end the war in their favor, Washington instead maneuvered his forces, continually striking hard and fast and unexpectedly at the places where the British least anticipated an attack.

The Battle of Trenton

Washington achieved a spectacular surprise success at Trenton on December 26, 1776. He gathered his men and had them row across the Delaware in the middle of the night. They attacked the Hessian garrison at sunrise while the men were still drunk and sleepy from their Christmas celebrations the night before. Washington was successful at maneuvering because he was able to think outside the box. Instead of fighting his battles in a traditional manner, he used guerilla tactics.

Later, using the same guerilla tactics, he successfully wiped out a British column on the road to Princeton. Eventually, with the help of the French, he pushed the British back into the peninsula at Yorktown and brought the war to a close. His ability to continually maneuver and innovate in the midst of a war was the key to victory.

Alexander the Great achieved his victories by maneuvering his cavalry and infantry in such a way that cracks opened up in the enemy lines through which he plunged with his elite cavalry, killing or driving off the opposing general and demoralizing the attacking forces.

Think Outside the Box

People have a natural tendency to fall in love with their own ideas, and with the ways of doing things to which they have become accustomed. Psychologists call this your "comfort zone." A basic rule in psychology says that you seek to get into a comfort zone, or a familiar routine, and once you are in it, you struggle and argue to stay there. If, for any reason, you are pushed out of your comfort zone by external circumstances, you immediately make every effort to re-create the comfort zone that you just left.

When you take a one- or two-week vacation, you often take your favorite pillow and coffee mug with you. When you arrive at your destination, you go down to the store and buy all the same foods that you were eating at home. You quickly re-create your comfort zone and adjust your lifestyle to your time of going to bed and getting up and to your daily rituals. You organize your life so that you feel comfortable doing the same things that you always do.

Creating a domestic or family comfort zone is healthy, natural, and positive. But getting into a comfort zone at work, especially when it causes you to resist change of any kind, can be harmful to your future. To escape the lure of the comfort zone, you must stay open to new ways of achieving the same goal and be willing to try new approaches when the old ways of doing things don't seem to be working anymore.

The rule is this: "Be clear about your goal or objective, but be *flexible* about how you achieve it."

Always be open to the possibility that your current strategy is either completely wrong or not as good as another strategy that you may have not yet considered. Be *flexible* so that you can adapt easily in critical situations. Be open to input from all sources. Ask people for their ideas. Read everything you can in your field. Attend every trade show, seminar, and conference that your professional organization puts together. Make a habit of attending meetings and associating with other people in your business, and related businesses. One new idea is all you need to start or build a fortune.

Develop Your Creativity

Ideas are your keys to the future. One new idea can change the entire direction of your life or your business. One breakthrough can completely change the focus of your company. One flash of insight, from yourself or from someone else, can open a door of opportunity that will enable your business to grow ten or twenty times in the years ahead. You must continually remain open to these ideas and flashes of insight in everything you do.

There are *four* excellent methods you can use to generate creative ideas and increase your maneuverability so that you can win in every business battle. These are the kaizen strategy, nominal group technique, mindstorming, and brainstorming. Each of these are idea generating strategies that you can practice both personally and in your company to increase the amount of originality and the level of innovation in your business.

The Kaizen Strategy of Continuous Betterment

W. Edwards Deming developed and introduced his quality improvement methods into Japanese manufacturing in the 1960s and 1970s. In two decades, Japanese products, which had been referred to as "Jap scrap," became synonymous with "quality" and "superb engineering." These quality improvement methods took Japan from a country that had been completely destroyed in 1945 to the number-two economic power in the world within one generation. This transformation was built on the Japanese process called "kaizen" which means "continuous betterment," or "continuous improvement."

Each employee of every Japanese company is encouraged to look for improvements that they can make in their "line of sight." What the Japanese found, and what you will find within your own business, is that there are always little things that can be done to improve quality or to increase efficiency in virtually every job. These improvements help the company adapt to changes in the market or in technology. Analogous to the principle of maneuver, the kaizen strategy keeps the staff of a company constantly on the alert to changing situations. These opportunities for improvement are usually right in front of you, right in your line of sight. They may be very small ways to increase efficiency taken one idea at a time, but the cumulative effect of hundreds and then thousands of little improvements, "continuous betterment" can lead to extraordinary increases in efficiency and productivity over time.

The kaizen technique is applied at every level of Japanese business and industry, from the entry-level employee sweeping the dock to the highest level executive running a worldwide business. What makes the technique effective is that each person is encouraged to try out his or her ideas on a small scale. There is seldom any need to get permission or authorization from a senior manager. The improvement can be quickly tested and modified right there at the workplace. If it is a successful modification, the results are shared with similar employees throughout the company. And the process never stops.

Look around you at your work. Where do opportunities exist for you to cut costs, increase the speed of an activity or process, reduce inefficiencies, or improve quality? Remember the song "Little Things Mean a Lot"? It is the same with continuous improvement. Hundreds and thousands of small improvements, spread over months and years, add up to an extraordinarily successful and profitable business. They mean a lot in terms of reduced costs and increased profits.

Nominal Group Technique
This is one of the most powerful creative thinking tools of all. It is simple, effective, and easy to use. You begin by creating a partial sentence that requires you to complete the statement.

Here is an example: "We could double our sales if . . . ." You complete this sentence with as many different ideas as you can think of.

You could use a statement like this: "We could double the number of referrals that we get from our customers if we only . . . ." How would you complete this sentence? Sit everyone down around the table and commit to generating at least twenty answers to the statement. The quality of the ideas generated by this technique is often amazing.

Once you have developed a few good answers, resolve to take action on at least one of those ideas immediately. Try it out. See what happens. Get feedback, and make corrections. Often the original idea will need to be modified to work effectively. One great idea to double your sales or your referrals can lead to an enormous surge in business and profitability.

Mindstorming

This is an exercise you can do by yourself. Take a sheet of paper and write your goal or problem at the top of the page in the form of a question.

Then discipline yourself to write twenty answers to your question. You absolutely refuse to stop until you have a minimum of twenty answers.

This is harder than you think. The first three to five answers will be fairly easy. But the next five answers will be harder, and the last ten answers may be so difficult that you will feel an irresistible urge to give up on the whole exercise.

But here's the good news. The first time you write twenty answers to a goal or problem phrased as a *question*, it will be difficult, like working out physically after a long time off. But the next time you use this method, you will generate twenty answers to whatever question you pose much faster. By the third time, you will find it easier and easier. Soon, you will be able to use this method to generate at least twenty answers (and sometimes thirty or forty answers) to any question or problem you have. And the quality of the answers will delight you.

Once you have completed your list of at least twenty answers, select the most obvious answer and take action on it immediately. This is important. It seems that taking action on one of your ideas keeps the ideas flowing. This exercise stimulates your creativity, and acting on your ideas keeps your creativity going hour after hour.

If you get up in the morning and write your major definite purpose as a question at the top of the page and then generate twenty answers to that question, you will be creative all day long. You will feel as if you have just done a series of vigorous aerobic mental exercises, which you have. Your mind will sparkle with ideas, insights, and solutions for hours afterward.

If you practiced mindstorming only five days per week and didn't even think on the weekends you would generate at least a hundred ideas per week. If you practiced mindstorming fifty weeks per year and didn't even think on your summer vacation you would generate 5,000 ideas per year (5 x 20 x 50 = 5,000).

If you then applied just one idea per day, five days per week, fifty weeks per year, you would be implementing 250 new ideas every year (1 x 5 x 50 = 250) to help you achieve your goals. Do you think that would have an effect on your results? You bet it would!

You would soon become one of the brightest and most creative people in your business. Each time you do this exercise, you will become even smarter and more creative. You will soon have so many good ideas to improve your life and work that you will not have enough hours in the day to try them all.

Tap the Brainpower of the Group

Brainstorming is one of the most powerful creative thinking exercises that a group of people can engage in together. Many companies and groups that have used brainstorming have achieved successes beyond the imagination of any of the participants. So can you.

Brainstorming is quite simple. You conduct it with a group of four to seven people. This seems to be the ideal number for idea generation.

You then create a clear question that demands practical answers. Discuss and agree on the question so that everyone is comfortable with the wording. The simpler the question, the better will be the quality of the answers.

For example, you could ask, "How can we cut our costs of operation by 20 percent over the next ninety days?" This question is clear, precise, specific, measurable, and time-bounded. It is the kind of question that generates the very best quality and quantity of answers and ideas.

The key to effective brainstorming is to focus on the *quantity* of answers rather than the *quality*. During the brainstorming session, you encourage everyone to contribute as many answers as possible to the question. Have one person record all the ideas for evaluation and review at a later time.

No ridicule, criticism, or comment is allowed on any idea unless it is positive and encouraging. The fastest way to cut off the flow of ideas is for someone to criticize something that someone else has said. As the leader of the brainstorming session, your job is to make sure that the environment is positive, optimistic, and cheerful. The more ridiculous ideas and laughter, the more successful the brainstorming session will be, and the better the resulting ideas will be. The goal is to get as many ideas as possible and not worry about whether or not some of them sound silly.

The Gulf War

In the Gulf War of 1991, General Norman Schwarzkopf used the principle of maneuver in his famous "Hail Mary" attack. After eliminating the ability of the Iraqi army to get accurate intelligence on the movement of his army, he moved what appeared to be a large force up to the Kuwaiti border. The Iraqi army moved forward to meet the expected attack.

Meanwhile, under the cover of night, General Schwarzkopf had moved 250,000 troops fifty miles to the west. At the critical moment, they launched a sweeping flank attack around the Iraqi forces, cutting them off at Basra and effectively ending the Gulf War. By destroying the enemy's ability to get accurate intelligence, Schwarzkopf was able to end the war quickly and effectively. He concentrated on reducing the time necessary to win the war and came up with the single most effective maneuver.

A Rocket to the Moon

In 1962, John F. Kennedy pledged that the United States would put a man on the moon and bring him safely back to earth within ten years. This was an enormous undertaking and was a response to the success of the Soviet Sputnik rockets orbiting the earth. The entire country rose up in a massive commitment to achieve this extraordinary goal.

In the nineteenth century, Jules Verne wrote a popular science-fiction novel entitled *From the Earth to the Moon*. In this book, he described a craft that took off from the earth, landed on the moon, and then took off from the moon and returned to the earth. This fictional account became the model that the engineers and designers at the National Aeronautics and Space Administration (NASA) used as their theoretical basis for the design of the moon rocket.

However, a problem quickly arose. For a rocket to break the earth's gravity, it would require many thousands of pounds of rocket fuel. When the rocket landed on the moon, it would again require many thousands of pounds of fuel to break the gravity of the moon and return to earth. The problem was, if the rocket carried enough fuel to break the moon's gravity once it got there, it would be too heavy to break the gravity of the earth and take off in the first place. The engineers had a real dilemma.

During a brainstorming session, one of the engineers threw out the idea, "Why does the rocket have to land on the moon in the first place?"

The chief design engineer asked him, "What do you mean, exactly?"

The engineer sketched out his idea. "What if we landed only a small part of the rocket on the moon?" he asked. "A small part of the rocket or module would only require a small amount of fuel to break the moon's gravity."

This was the breakthrough that led to the lunar module, piloted by Buzz Aldrin and under the command of Neil Armstrong, that landed on the moon in 1969. Instead of attempting to land the entire rocket on the moon, the crew dropped a small module to the moon while the main rocket stayed in orbit, conserving its fuel for the return journey to earth. At the appropriate time, the lunar module took off from the moon, rejoined the orbiting space ship, and they flew back to earth together.

This breakthrough idea led to the U.S. success in space and the moon landing, something that has never been equaled by any other power, including the Soviets. The Americans won the space race through superior technology and sheer ingenuity. One idea from one engineer in one brainstorming session literally changed the direction of the entire U.S. space program.

The principle of maneuver, expressed in innovation, originality, and creative thinking, continually seeking new, better, faster, and easier ways to achieve the objective, is the key to your success, both today and for the indefinite future.

Like a muscle, your creative abilities improve the more you use them. The more you practice thinking and acting creatively, the more and better ideas you will come up with from all sources. You will eventually reach the point in your mind where you know that there is no goal that you cannot achieve, no objective that you cannot seize, and no problem that you cannot solve by using the creative capabilities of your own mind.

The Principle of Maneuver in Personal Success

There are three triggers to personal creativity: 1) intensely desired goals; 2) pressing problems; and 3) focused questions. You should use all three of these to keep your personal creativity functioning at a high level.

Perhaps the most important conclusion, reached by the greatest thinkers of history, is that "You become what you think about most of the time."

Thought is creative. You create and maintain your world with your own thinking. As Shakespeare wrote in *Hamlet*, " . . . for there is nothing either good or bad but thinking makes it so." You do not see the world as it is, but as you are. You give the meaning, significance, and importance to everything around you. Without your thinking the thought, nothing in your world has any relevance to you. Descartes said, "I think, therefore I am."

The law of concentration says that "Whatever you dwell on grows and increases in your world." Whenever you concentrate your thoughts on any subject, you attract more ideas, people, and resources on that subject into your life. When you become preoccupied or obsessed with a thought, you say and do more and more things that work together to make that thought a reality.

Successful, happy people think about what they *want* most of the time. Unsuccessful people, unfortunately, think and talk about the things they don't want most of the time. Successful people get more and more of the things that they want faster and faster, while unsuccessful people get more of the things they don't want. In either case, the law is working.

When you continually think and talk about how you can achieve your most intensely desired goals, you will find more and more ways to move toward your goals faster and faster.

When you clearly identify your most pressing problems and continually seek for solutions using some of the creative thinking tools discussed earlier in this chapter you will come up with idea after idea to help you move ahead faster.

When you ask yourself focused questions about your situation, your life, and your work, you provoke and trigger more and better answers that help you to make better decisions.

The greater clarity you have with regard to your goals, your problems, and the questions you can ask to help you analyze and achieve them better and faster, the brighter and more creative you will be. Just as you become physically fit by working out physically, you become mentally fit by practicing these exercises and working out mentally.

The Island-Hopping Campaign

General Douglas McArthur used his famous "Island-Hopping Strategy" to achieve victory in the Pacific. Beginning in 1942, the Japanese invested huge amounts of men and matériel fortifying the Solomon Islands chain, which leads from Australia north to the Philippines. They expected the American armed forces to exhaust themselves attacking and defeating the garrisons dug in on each of these islands.

Instead, McArthur simply bypassed the fortified islands and cut them off from resupply. In effect, he left the large Japanese garrisons "dangling in the wind" while he focused and concentrated on the few islands that were essential to the re-conquest of the Pacific. McArthur focused on the solution—rather than taking on the Japanese forces, he used a much more effective method that produced the same results.

The ability of great generals throughout the ages to adapt and apply the principle of maneuver to the rapidly changing conditions around them has been a major factor in their victories time and time again. Focusing on the desired solution rather than the process helps you adapt more easily to changing circumstances while still achieving the desired results.

Practice Solution-Orientation

General Colin Powell said in a recent interview, "I believe that leadership is the ability to solve problems." Your ability to solve problems is the critical determinant of your success or failure in life. This ability makes you a leader in your own life. And a goal unachieved is merely a problem you have not yet solved.

You rise in life to the height of the problems that you have demonstrated an ability to solve effectively. The better you get at solving problems, the bigger and more important problems you will be given to solve. As you solve bigger and more complex problems, your prestige, respect, and rewards will increase commensurately.

The key to becoming an excellent problem solver, in whatever field, is to think about *solutions* all the time. The more you think and talk about possible solutions, the more possible solutions will come to you. The more solutions you come up with, the faster and easier it becomes for you to solve even more problems in the future.

Only about 10 percent of the population thinks about solutions *most* of the time. The great majority think and talk about their problems, who is to blame, and what the problems are going to cost. They often feel helpless in the face of problems and wish and hope that someone else will come along and solve the problems for them.

The most important word you can learn, for the rest of your life, is the word "How?" This is the key word for problem solving and creative thinking. Whenever you have a goal that you have not yet achieved, the only question you ask is "How?" How can you achieve the goal? What are all the different things that you can do? What steps can you take immediately? What is the next step?

When you have a problem of any kind, your only question is "How?" How can we solve it? How can we overcome the obstacle? How can we resolve the difficulty, remove the road-block, or alleviate the constraint?

Any question that begins with the word "How?" stimulates your creativity. It forces you to be solution-oriented. It puts you in control of your own thinking. It gives you energy and centers you in your work. The question "How?" empowers you and puts you back in charge of the situation. All leaders think in terms of "how"

The Principle of Maneuver Revisited

You have heard it said that "The more you do of what you're doing, the more you'll get of what you've got." All originality and innovation, all progress, come from doing things differently from the way they have been done in the past. In the King James version of the Bible, it says, " . . . Seek, and ye shall find; knock, and it shall be opened unto you." What this means in business terms is that if you look for newer, better, faster, cheaper ways to overcome your obstacles and achieve your goals, you will almost always find them.

The habit of continuous creativity, flexibility, and the practice of the principle of maneuver in dealing with turbulent situations and a rapidly changing market will give you the winning edge over your competitors. By moving quickly on insights and ideas, you eventually become unstoppable.

CHAPTER FIVE

The Principle of Intelligence
Get the Facts!

Know the enemy and know yourself; in a hundred battles you will never be in peril. When you are ignorant of the enemy but know yourself, your chances of winning or losing are equal. If ignorant both of your enemy and of yourself, you are certain in every battle to be in peril.

—SUN TZU, ANCIENT CHINESE GENERAL

The more you know about what you are doing, the better decisions you can make and the more effective you will be. Great military and business leaders are continually gathering and sorting information, seeking those key insights and ideas that can give them the advantage in a tight contest.

The Enigma Machine

The German Army in 1941 was the most formidable army in the world. Its policy of blitzkrieg or "lightning war," using tanks and

101

armored personnel carriers, had enabled it to conquer Poland in 1939 and then much of Eastern Europe in a few weeks. Denmark, Norway, Belgium, the Netherlands, and Luxembourg were all forced to surrender to the Germans in the spring of 1940. In May of 1940, by attacking unexpectedly through the Ardennes in Belgium, which the Allies had thought to be impenetrable, the German Army split France in two, scattered the Allied armies, and drove the survivors back to the English Channel. In the heroic Operation Dynamo, 338,226 troops, including about 100,000 French soldiers, were evacuated from the port of Dunkirk in early June. But there were more than two million French casualties, and the British lost 11,000 troops with an additional 50,000 wounded or taken prisoner. By the end of June 1940, France had fallen, something that had not happened in four bitter years of trench warfare in World War I.

The German U-boats were devastating shipping in the North Atlantic. In 1941, German armies were moving unopposed through Yugoslavia and into Greece. The Deutsches Afrika Korps was being formed under Field Marshal Erwin Rommel for action in Tunisia. The German forces seemed unstoppable.

As the result of twenty years of demilitarization, appeasement, and the outright refusal of the British or French to see the emerging Nazi threat, the British especially were woefully unprepared. Meanwhile, the German war machine consisted of hundreds of thousands of trained soldiers supported by thousands of tanks and armored vehicles as well as thousands of fighter and bomber aircraft.

The Germans also had a secret weapon, the Enigma machine. This incredibly sophisticated device allowed the Germans to communicate worldwide with a code that was impossible to break. Each encoded message was encrypted differently from each subsequent message when it was run through the Enigma machine. Because of this, there was no consistent code to be broken by the Allied powers. The German intelligence services and military commanders could send and receive top-secret messages worldwide with no fear of detection.

However, an incredibly fortunate event took place early in the war. The Allies were able to obtain an Enigma machine and secretly transport it into England. The existence of this machine in Allied intelligence became one of the biggest secrets of the war and was not revealed until well after the war was over.

The Allies set up a separate intelligence unit at a large estate called Bletchley Park forty miles north of London. This unit was fully staffed by intelligence experts with the highest top-secret clearances possible in the Allied military. These code-breakers and translators worked day and night throughout the entire war intercepting German communications, deciphering them, and making them available to the key commanders and relevant parties.

This intelligence breakthrough was a major reason for the Allied victory in Europe. The capture of an Enigma machine and the codebooks that went with it gave the Allies a critical edge that enabled them to ultimately prevail over a formidable military force. This was a superb example of the value of good intelligence in warfare.

Sometimes, one piece of information is all that is necessary to give the advantage to one force or the other. The gathering, acquisition, and interpretation of military intelligence is a key to victory in all battles and campaigns.

> **THE PRINCIPLE OF INTELLIGENCE:**
> Do everything possible to determine the dispositions,
> plans, strengths, and weaknesses of the enemy, plus
> know the terrain and all other factors that could affect
> the outcome of the engagement.

Use every method possible to gather and accurately inter-
pret information that will enable you to better plan for, prepare, and defeat the enemy.

The Principle of Intelligence in Business

The more and better information you have about your competition and your market, the better decisions you can make and
the more likely you are to be successful. Excellent commanders and business leaders are continually acquiring more and
better information that they can use to improve the quality of
their decisions affecting business operations. One piece of new
and unexpected information can immediately change the competitive situation and alter your way of doing business. It can
give you a unique advantage.

All business strategy is aimed at acquiring and keeping customers. The primary limitation on your ability to acquire and
keep all the customers you want is the actions of your competitors, the same companies that are after the customers that
you want yourself.

Know Your Competitors

The starting point of competitive intelligence gathering is for you
to be absolutely clear about your *ideal* customer. You must know

exactly what it is you sell and the person to whom you sell it. You must have carefully thought through the issues of *specialization, differentiation, segmentation, concentration, and positioning.* You must know and understand your market completely and keep adding to your storehouse of market knowledge.

Based on this information, who are your *competitors*? Who are the other individuals or organizations that are attempting to get the same dollar that you want from the same customer?

This question forces you to answer three questions: First, why should anybody buy your product at all? What are the primary values or benefits that a customer would be seeking if he were to be a qualified prospect for you or for anyone else selling a similar product?

The second question is: Once a customer has decided to buy the type of product or service you offer, why should that customer buy it from you? Just because the prospect is qualified to buy what you sell does not mean that the prospect will buy it from you or from your company. You have to be crystal clear as to why the prospect would choose you over any other organization or individual offering something similar.

The third question you must answer is: What is your area of excellence? What is your competitive advantage? What is it that your product or service offers a customer that makes it superior to any other competing product or service available? The answer to this question becomes the focal point of all your advertising, marketing, and sales efforts. It dictates the structure of your sales presentation and becomes the driving force of all your marketing activities.

The greater accuracy you can develop with regard to your competitors, the more capable you will be of planning an effective marketing strategy. A change in the definition of your competitor or your competitive advantage can actually change the entire focus of your business.

The Battle of Midway

The Japanese fleet under Admiral Isoroku Yamamoto was eager to destroy the American aircraft carriers that had escaped destruction at Pearl Harbor. In June 1942, the Japanese chose to attack the islands of Midway in the Central Pacific to draw out the American fleet. What Yamamoto did not know was that U.S. Navy codebreakers had achieved a breakthrough, solving the Japanese fleet codes. This enabled Pacific Fleet Commander Admiral Chester W. Nimitz to understand the exact Japanese plans as they were formulated.

For several weeks, American radio operators picked up various orders from Admiral Yamamoto to his various forces, preparing for the battle. When the battle began, Admiral Nimitz had reconstructed the Japanese plans in order of battle in considerable detail. The results were disastrous for the Japanese. The Americans sank four aircraft carriers, the *Akagi*, *Kaga*, *Soryu*, and *Hiryu*, the entire strength of the task force, plus the heavy cruiser *Mikuma*. The Japanese lost 322 aircraft and over 5,000 sailors. The American losses included 147 aircraft and more than 300 seamen.

Many historians view Midway as the turning point in the Pacific War. This success was due to the combination of excellent military intelligence and superb American naval power.

Löwenbräu

Many years ago, the makers of the German beer Löwenbräu tried to break into the U.S. market by competing against American beers. But no matter how much or how clever the advertising, the sales of Löwenbräu remained low. Then one day, a copywriter for the advertising agency came up with an idea. Why not reposition the beer, choose a different competitor, and change the entire strategy of the marketing campaign.

The next month, the first new advertisements for Löwenbräu appeared. They said, "When you run out of Champagne, order Löwenbräu."

The sales of Löwenbräu took off from that day forward and Löwenbräu has been a top selling imported beer in the United States ever since. By changing the focus and defining Löwenbräu as a drink that has the same status as Champagne rather than as a competitor with lower-priced American beers, they created a multi-million dollar market overnight.

Analyze Yourself Over Your Competitors

Create a competitive analysis grid comparing yourself and your products and services to each one of your competitors. Be brutally honest with yourself. Rate yourself on a scale of one to ten, with one being the lowest and ten being the highest on every measure. Ask other people inside and outside of your company how they would rate you on these particular scales in comparison with competitors.

Here are some questions you can ask: What is the size of your company in comparison to your competitors? How long have you been in business? What is your sales volume? Are you a local company or a national company? Do you have branches in other countries? How do your competitors measure up to you in these areas?

Perhaps the most important question has to do with your reputation. What is the quality of your reputation in the marketplace? If researchers were to ask several hundred or several thousand customers how they rated you against your competitors, where would you appear in the quality rankings?

According to the PIMS studies at Harvard, which examined 620 companies over twenty years, the company that is rated as the "highest quality" in its industry will almost always be the most profitable company in that industry as well. How would you rate your offerings in terms of quality in comparison with your competitors? Are you number one? Number two? Number ten?

Whatever your answer, ask yourself, "How could we improve our rankings? What could we do to move up in the scale of 'quality perception' among the customers in our market?" This is a key question for strategic planning and organizational development.

How do the prices of your offerings compare to that of your competitors? Are your prices higher or lower? Why or why not? Sometimes, changing your pricing structure relative to your competitors can change your position in the market completely.

What quality of people do you have in comparison with your competitors? Do you have better or worse leadership and management? Are your marketing and sales efforts better or worse? How does your customer service compare with that of your competitors on a scale of one to ten?

One of the most important actions you can take is to conduct a regular *customer satisfaction survey* asking as many of your customers as possible what they think about you and what you would have to do to get more business from them. Our company regularly conducts customer satisfaction surveys for our clients. The results are often eye-opening, if not astonishing. This type of market intelligence can lead to your completely changing the way you advertise, market, sell, and do business.

In what ways are your products or services superior to those of your competitors? In what specific areas do you offer greater value than anyone else? Why should a customer buy from you rather than from a rival company?

In what areas are your competitors superior to you? What are they doing right? What are they doing that enables them to sell more of their products or services to the same customers that you are trying to sell to?

One of the most important attitudes you develop in warfare is to *respect* your adversary. Never take him for granted. Always assume that he is intelligent and competent. Assume that he is thinking every minute about how to defeat you, just as you are thinking about how to defeat him.

In business, you should always *admire* your successful competitors. Whenever they do something original or effective in the market that enables them to get business that you want for yourself, stand back and study their successes. Try to learn from them. The more you admire your successful competitors, the more you will emulate what it is they are doing well, and eventually surpass them.

What are the *strengths* of your competitors compared to you? What are their weaknesses in comparison to you? What are the threats to their business that you can exploit? What are the opportunities open to them that you can preclude by rapid action?

Finally, how does your sales force stack up against that of your competitors? In the final analysis, your ability to sell well is the critical determinant of your success or failure in any market. Sometimes, upgrading your sales force and refocusing your sales efforts can revolutionize your entire business. Could this be a possible strategy for you?

Perception Is Reality

In military strategy, the commander relies upon his perception of the relative strength and disposition of the forces against him. One of the rules of military intelligence, especially in the area of espionage, is to influence and shape this perception advantageously. By inducing the enemy commander to believe that you are massing your troops for an attack on a particular objective, you can cause him to move his forces forward to defend at that point. You can then attack successfully in an area that is now relatively undefended.

Each company and each individual is positioned in a particular way in the hearts and minds of other people. The way that your customers, present and future, think about you when your name is mentioned is the critical determinant of whether or not they buy from you.

The customer's perception is the customer's *reality*. The truth of the situation, or your product, service, or company, does not matter. All that matters is what the customer thinks and feels about you when you are not there.

One of the great rules for success in life is: "Everything counts!" Every customer contact or customer experience either helps you or hurts you. Everything either leads toward a sale or leads away from one. Everything counts!

One of the most important parts of market intelligence is determining in advance how you want to position yourself relative to your customers, just as a military commander decides how he wants to position his forces relative to the enemy.

How do you want people to think and talk about you? What are the steps that you can take—starting from the first phone call to your office through to the follow-up service on your delivered product or service—that you can change to improve the perception your customers have of you?

Each of these questions is important. If you change your answer to any one of these questions from what you are doing today, this new answer can lead to a complete change of marketing strategy in your business. At the very least, everyone responsible for sales and profitability in your company should know the answers to every one of the questions above. Everyone should have a clear, uncomplicated idea of who you are, why you are in business, and why people should buy from you rather than from someone else.

The Battle of Bokhara

In 1220, Genghis Khan led his Mongol army in a campaign against Shah Mohammed to conquer his Khwarazm Empire, a huge landmass that covered much of modern-day Iran, Uzbekistan, Tajikistan, Afghanistan, and Turkmenistan. The key to victory was the capture of the fortified capital city of Bokhara.

Shah Mohammed had more than 200,000 men spread out in garrisons along the Jaxartes River in the cities of Tashkent, Kohkand, and Samarkand. Bokhara was defended from all directions except the north. The vast Kyzyl Kum Desert in what is now Kazakhstan and Uzbekistan effectively blocked invasion from that direction and was known to be impassable.

In one of the great intelligence maneuvers of history, Genghis Khan moved north from Utrar and captured a Turkoman city, Zarnuk, for the sole purpose of acquiring a man who had lived in the Kyzyl Kum Desert all his life and knew where the oases were located. The knowledge of this one man enabled the Mongol army to cross the desert from one water hole to another and fall upon the largely unguarded capital city of Bokhara from the rear.

With Bokhara captured, the Khwarazm Empire was cut in half. Shah Mohammed was in the field at Tashkent in the east and could not raise troops from west of Bokhara. He was effectively deprived of his capital. He came under immediate assault by two other Mongol armies attacking him from the north and east. His army lost confidence in him and soon went over to the Mongols.

Shah Mohammed fled for his life, losing his entire empire and dying of pleurisy on a small island in the Caspian Sea a year later. Genghis Khan had conquered one of the richest empires of the ancient and medieval world through cunning, deception, speed, and the excellent use of military intelligence. He also knew the value of other people's intelligence and unique knowledge.

Knowledge Is the Primary Source of Value

Just as Genghis Khan understood the value of one man's knowledge, you must understand that your people are your most valuable assets. It is the knowledge and skill between the ears of your key people that represents the most valuable part of your business. Your business walks out the door every day at five o'clock. You could lose every tangible asset—furniture, fixtures, buildings, cars, files, computers, and everything else—but as long as you kept your key people, you could be back in business again tomorrow, generating sales and making profits. As Colin Powell said, "Those people in the field are closest to the problem, closest to the situation; therefore, that is where the real wisdom is."

There are three types of knowledge that a business needs to survive and thrive. In Thomas Stewart's wonderful book *Intellectual Capital*, he defines these forms of knowledge as personal knowledge, company knowledge, and market knowledge.

Personal knowledge is the specific knowledge, skills, education, background, experience, training, and core competencies that an individual owns and takes with her from place to place. The ability to write, to speak publicly, to negotiate, to sell, to make presentations, to type, to prepare financial statements, and so on, are all forms of personal intellectual capital. The more of these kinds of knowledge and skills that are relevant to your business a person has, the more valuable that person can be.

The process of interviewing and selection, as well as delegation, supervision, and promotion, revolves around the determination and deployment of these core skills.

The second type of knowledge is the knowledge of your specific company. This form of intellectual capital is very valuable. This includes knowledge about the processes and procedures within your business, the key personalities and their relationships to each other, your products and services and how they are developed, sold, and delivered, and all the other unique factors and features that make your business different from any other.

When a person works for a business for any time, that person absorbs an enormous amount of valuable information about how that business functions. This heightened knowledge and awareness has a real value. If you lose a person who is intimately familiar with many aspects of your business, the cost of hiring and training a new person to the same level of competence can be very high.

The third type of intellectual capital is specific knowledge about your market, your customers, and your competitors; and about your products and services, and the way they are marketed, sold, and delivered. This kind of customer and market knowledge can be of inestimable value in a competitive marketplace. The longer a salesperson, for example, works for a company, the more valuable he becomes in terms of his network of contacts and his intimate knowledge of customers—who they are, where they are, why they buy, and the various buying influences that operate on them.

Not long ago, a client company of mine brought in a new controller. This controller looked over the payroll and arbitrarily decided that the top salesman was earning too much money. He insisted to the president that the salesman's commission be cut, his territory be reduced, and several of his major clients be turned into "house accounts."

As it happened, this salesman represented about 40 percent of the total sales of this medium-sized manufacturing company. When they told him that they were going to cut his commissions and cut his territories, thereby reducing his income by more than 50 percent, he protested. He said, "This is not fair! I have spent twelve years building up my customer base. You can't just take it away from me like this."

They refused to listen. The controller said, "In reality, these customers belong to the company, not to you. Their loyalty is to us and to our products and services. There is no reason we should continue to pay you so much money to service accounts that actually belong to us. If you're not happy with these new arrangements, you can go somewhere else."

The salesman tried to reason with them, but to no avail. Finally, he quit and walked across the street to their major competitor, taking all the accounts with him. His old company's sales dropped 38 percent the following year. They almost went bankrupt. They had no idea that the relationship between the salesman and his customers was perhaps the most valuable form of intellectual capital in the entire company.

There Is No Substitute for Victory

Your goal is to win customers in a competitive market. Your goal is to be superior to your competitors. Your goal is to achieve victory against whatever odds you are facing. This means that you must continually examine and re-examine every part of your competitive posture, continually looking for ways to achieve superiority relative to your competitors.

Every day in every way, you must be looking for faster, better, cheaper, and easier ways for your customers to do business with you. You must be continually improving your product or service offerings. You must be watching your competitors like a hawk and quickly copying them when they introduce an innovation or improvement. Continually learning and upgrading your knowledge leads to the better deployment of your resources, thereby increasing your productivity or effectiveness.

As Tom Peters wrote in *In Search of Excellence*, "The very best companies act as though they are on the verge of losing every single customer, every single day." This is a great philosophy of customer relations and customer service for you to copy.

The Navajo Code Talkers

In the Pacific, after considerable effort and the application of many of the most brilliant minds in America, the American intelligence services were able to break the Japanese military codes. As a result, they were able to anticipate many of the moves of the Japanese navy and air force in the Pacific theater.

One captured message in 1943 revealed the exact time and place that Admiral Yamamoto, the Commander-in-Chief of the Japanese Combined Fleet who was the architect of the attack at Pearl Harbor and perhaps the most important military commander in the Japanese armed forces, would be flying on a tour of inspection. With this information, the American navy was able to send out fighter interceptors, shoot down his plane, and eliminate a key enemy commander in the Pacific War.

Meanwhile, in order to thwart the Japanese attempts to break the American codes, the U.S. military made an interesting discovery. They found that the Navajo language was only known by a few thousand people in the world, mostly residents of Arizona. It was not even a written language and was unknown to anyone outside of the United States. They came up with the brilliant idea of having all of their radio communications in the Pacific sent and received in the Navajo language, using Navajo speakers from Arizona and New Mexico on every ship. From 1941 until the end of the war, the Japanese could never figure out what they were saying.

The Principle of Intelligence in Personal Success

At one time, the great division in society was between those who "had more" and those who "had less." Today the primary difference is between those who "know more" and those who "know less." Here is the rule: "Your life only gets better when you get better."

Knowledge and know-how are your keys to the twenty-first century. The more accurate information and knowledge that you acquire and apply to achieve results, the more valuable you will become. The greater your value, the more you will be paid and the faster you will be promoted. Just as the Navajo Indians knew a unique language that helped the United States win World War II, sometimes knowing a special skill or having unique knowledge gives you the winning edge. The good news is that there is no limit to how much more knowledge you can acquire or how much better you can become by your own efforts. There is therefore no limit on how much you can improve your life. It is entirely up to you, and you are responsible.

Verdun

In the fall of 1916, the French launched a major offensive at Verdun, driving the Germans back and winning a major victory. The following spring, the French attempted a similar but larger offensive against the Germans and were defeated with terrible casualties. What was the difference?

In one of the major tactical innovations of the war, the Germans had quickly developed a sophisticated system utilizing artillery, fire power, and movement to dominate the battlefield. They had learned from their mistakes, compensated for their weaknesses, and were prepared to both attack and counter attack effectively against the French armies.

This principle of intelligence, continually gathering new information, adapting and adjusting to changing circumstances, and then taking offensive action in the pursuit of goals and objectives is even more important in business today. And it is a never ending process.

Leaders Are Learners

Leaders are *learners*. Today, lifelong learning is the minimum requirement for success in your field or any field. With knowledge and information doubling every three to five years, your personal knowledge about your field must be doubling every three to five years as well just to stay even.

Your goal should be to join the top 10 percent in your field. You should do an analysis of your field and determine what the people in the top 10 percent today are earning. You should then find out what it is they are doing to earn that kind of money. You can ask them directly and they will probably tell you. Whatever answers you get, follow up. Read the books, listen to the audio programs, and take the courses. Do what they do until you get the same results they get.

No one is better than you and no one is smarter than you. If someone is doing better than you at the moment, it is because they have learned and applied specialized knowledge and information faster than you have. And anything that anyone else has done, you can do as well. You just need to find out what it is.

Here are some questions you can ask: (1) What do you most enjoy about your current work? (2) What has been most responsible for your success in your career to date? (3) What do you do easily and well that seems to be difficult for others? (4) What part of your work most interests and fascinates you? (5) Of all the things you do, what contributes the greatest value to your work and your company? (6) If you could only do one thing all day long, what one thing would that be? (7) What one skill, if you developed and did it in an excellent fashion, would help you the most in your career? Keep asking these questions of yourself, your boss, and others. The answers will keep you focused on your most valuable tasks and continually growing in competence and ability.

The Battle of Tannenberg

At the Battle of Tannenberg in what was then East Prussia in August 1914, the Russian and German Armies were reasonably well matched in numbers of soldiers in the field. The battle opened with a Russian defeat of the German Eighth Army. Fortunately for Germany, the Russian First Army under General Pavel Rennenkampf did not follow-up on its success. This gave the Germans time to reorganize. The decisive factor in the battle was the Germans' ability to pick up the Russian wireless messages, which for some reason, were being transmitted in the clear and without encryption. Thus the Germans knew the Russian dispositions and plans and were able to attack and counterattack accordingly.

By the end of the battle, on August 30, 1914, the entire Russian Second Army was virtually wiped out. Ninety-two thousand men were taken prisoner, 30,000 were killed or missing, and some 400 artillery guns were lost.

Because of a major intelligence failure on the part of the Russians, the Battle of Tannenberg was lost, Russia was forced into a treaty with Germany and knocked out of the War. The collapse of Russian military and civilian morale that followed led to the Bolshevik Revolution in 1917, the fall of Czar Nicholas II and the royal family, and the emergence of Lenin and the Communists.

The Russians and Germans were relatively equal in terms of men in battle. The Germans were able to gain the advantage at a critical moment because they learned and applied specialized knowledge and information. In order to succeed, you also need to discover specialized knowledge and information that will give you the edge and use it to your advantage.

Your Most Valuable Financial Asset

Your most financially valuable asset is your *earning ability*. Your earning ability is the sum total of all the things that you can do to get results for other people. The more you increase your earning ability, the more valuable you become to yourself and others. And the more valuable you become, the more you will be paid, and the better the life you will have.

There are two types of people in our world, those who think in terms of monthly and annual income and those who think in terms of results. People who think in terms of their weekly, monthly, or annual paychecks almost invariably drift through the days, waste much of their time, socialize with their co-workers, come in late, and leave early. They are paid accordingly. And they don't have much of a chance in terms of dramatically increasing their income.

The top leaders and winners in life think exclusively in terms of *results*. They are continually asking, "What results are expected of me?" They value every minute of every day. They think in terms of earning their income on an hourly basis rather than weekly, monthly, or annual pay.

Here is an exercise for you: Determine the amount of money you want to earn over the next twelve months. Divide that amount of money by 2,000 hours, the average number of hours that you will work in a full year. If your goal is to earn $100,000 per year, divide that amount by 2,000 hours to get a desired hourly rate of fifty dollars per hour. (If your goal is $50,000 per year, your desired hourly rate would be twenty-five dollars per hour.)

From this point onward, make sure that you earn fifty dollars or more every single hour. Continually ask yourself, "Would I pay somebody else fifty dollars an hour to do what I'm doing right now?" If the answer is "no," stop doing it immediately and start doing something that pays fifty dollars an hour or more.

If you make a list of everything that you do at work, you will find that you only earn your desired hourly rate when you are doing two or three specific tasks that are the most valuable to your company. Your job is to organize your work life in such a way that you are working on those tasks all day long.

By the "Law of Sowing and Reaping," which says that you reap what you sow, you cannot make your own photocopies, drink coffee, read the paper, or do work that someone else would do for five or ten dollars an hour, and then expect to make fifty dollars an hour by the end of the year. This is not the way the world works.

Your most financially valuable asset is your earning ability, and your primary responsibility in life is to build your earning ability to the highest possible level by finding out what are the most valuable things you do and concentrating on those activities. If you do this, your financial future will be unlimited.

The Principle of Intelligence Revisited

Your mind is your most precious treasure, and your earning ability is you most valuable asset. The more you learn about how to be more effective and valuable to yourself and your company, the more you will earn and the better the life you will have.

Ideas and information, knowledge and know how, are the critical determinants of your success. There is no real limit to what you can learn to improve the quality of your life, so there is no real limit on your potential.

Today, life is a *race*, and you are in it, whether you like it or not. Your job is to win out against the competition, to use your incredible mind to solve your problems, overcome your obstacles, and achieve your goals. When you begin to tap regularly into your mental abilities, you will become unstoppable!

CHAPTER SIX

The Principle of Concerted Action

Coordinate Your Activities

I quickly learned that teamwork—all pulling together toward an identifiable common goal—worked far better than rushing headlong "over the top" only to discover that no one was behind you.

—ARTHUR OCHS SULZBERGER, SR., FORMER CAPTAIN IN THE

U.S. MARINE CORPS AND PUBLISHER OF THE NEW YORK TIMES

Teamwork, synergy, and coordination are essential to the success of any enterprise, military or business. One of the most important of all force multipliers is your ability to work harmoniously with the people around you. This enables you to accomplish vastly more than you could by yourself.

The Battle Of Chickamauga

A smaller military force, working with smoothness and speed, can destroy a much larger and less coordinated force. On September 18, 1863, a battle developed between the Union forces commanded by General William S. Rosecrans, Army of the Cumberland, and General Braxton Bragg's Confederate Army of Tennessee.

Overconfident as the result of several minor successes, Rosecrans spread his troops out along Chickamauga Creek in Georgia while Bragg concentrated his forces opposite him. Rosecrans mistakenly ordered a federal division out of the line just at the moment that a major attack in echelon led by General James Longstreet, hit the Union front.

Longstreet had lined up three divisions, one behind the other. The job of the first division was to break the line, the job of the second division was to exploit the breakthrough, and the job of the third division was to overwhelm the Union troops, breaking out in their rear, splitting the army and routing them in both directions.

The concept of "attacking in echelon" refers to the ability of a commander to bring his troops into action smoothly, one division after another, in sequence, in such a way that the enemy has no time to regroup or respond effectively.

At the Battle of Chickamauga, a Confederate victory, a massive Confederate column rushed through the gap created by Rosecrans's lack of coordination among his units. Thousands of Union troops broke under the attack and fled all the way back to Chattanooga. The failure to fight in a concerted fashion led to a major defeat while the concerted action of the Confederate army led to an unexpected victory.

The Mongol Army

The Mongol Tuman, or division, under Genghis Khan numbered 10,000 men. Each Mongol army was composed of two Tumans or 20,000 men. The Mongol army was always outnumbered by its enemies overall, but never outnumbered by its enemies at a specific point of battle. The unmatchable ability of the Mongol army under its generals to move smoothly and effectively made it the most formidable fighting force in the world at that time.

THE PRINCIPLE OF CONCERTED ACTION:
Unify and bring all elements of your forces to work
together simultaneously in the achievement of your aims.

Communicate clear objectives, goals, plans, and responsibilities to every unit, complete with deadlines and schedules of attack and coordination throughout the action.

The Principle of Concerted Action in Business

The highest act of leadership in business is the ability to bring together a group of high-performance individuals and concentrate their time, attention, and abilities on the achievement of business goals.

Concerted action is the key to the principle of *synergy*. In its simplest terms, synergy means that the total output of a group of people is vastly greater than the output of those same individuals working separately. In other words, two plus two does not equal four but rather six or eight or ten. A single person working alone may accomplish a certain amount. A well-coordinated team, working in concert, can accomplish vastly more.

Teamwork Is the Key to High Performance

In business today, all work is done by teams. Your ability to function well as part of a team, or as a team leader, is a critical factor in determining how far you go and how fast you get there. The most valued people in every company are those who are described as good team players.

The manager's work is actually the work of the team. The manager's results are the results that the team gets. By putting together a team, the manager can move from what she can do to what she can *control*. She can shift from operating to managing. She can concentrate all her attention on getting things done through others.

In the past, it was common to say, "If you want something done properly, you have to do it yourself."

Today however, this has been completely reversed. If you are serious about being successful in business today, what you say is "If you want something done properly, you have to find someone to do it."

It takes no brains or special talent to roll up your sleeves and do it yourself. But it takes real brains and ability to find and deploy the right person to do the job instead. This is where you must focus.

Great managers are great because they have staffed their companies with excellent people in every critical position. Great generals are great because they have excellent officers at every level of command. No one does it alone. Everyone needs the help of other talented people.

Operation Desert Sabre

In the 1991 Gulf War, after six months of detailed planning, General Norman Schwarzkopf launched the Desert Sabre ground offensive in a sweeping movement through the defenses of the Iraqi army. Every man and woman, every regiment, and every division had been told of the coming offensive in detail. Every officer knew exactly what he was supposed to do, and when, and where. The ground operation was virtually flawless. The army functioned like a Swiss watch with total unity and coordination from the firing of the first gun to the fall of Basra and the end of the Gulf War. It was a masterpiece of concerted action.

Smooth, well-coordinated action among military units is a *force multiplier.* A highly unified and well-coordinated force has hitting power vastly in excess of its numbers and can often disperse and destroy a superior force.

Five Keys to Peak Performance Teams

In a longitudinal study shared with me by one of my Fortune 500 clients, more than 120 teams were studied over a three-year period at a cost of several million dollars. These teams were selected because they had accomplished extraordinary results in terms of new product introductions, cost reductions, innovative business solutions, and the ability to get superb results. These peak-performing teams turned out to have five qualities in common.

1. Shared goals. Every team that achieved extraordinary results had shared goals. When they were given their assignments—to cut manufacturing costs, increase the speed of new product development, or expand market share—the first thing the top teams did was to sit down among themselves and get complete agreement on the goals toward which they were working.

Clarity is essential. The greater clarity people have with regard to their goals, the easier it is for them to commit whole-heartedly to achieving them. There is a direct relationship between participation in the discussion of goals and the commitment and determination of the team members to achieve those goals afterward.

If you announce a goal to your team, the goal remains your property. But if you involve the team by explaining and discussing the goal, the team takes ownership of the goal. They then become more creative in finding ways to achieve the goal, faster and more cheaply.

2. Shared values. The top-performing teams had shared values. Like the team goals, these were developed by discussion back and forth among the team members until everyone was in agreement.

With values like these, the teams worked together smoothly and got much more done.

3. Shared plans. The best teams had shared plans. Everyone knew the plan of action. In addition, everyone knew what each team member was expected to do and when and how accomplishments would be measured. The entire team managed by objectives. Team discussions were focused around the common goals, common values, and common plans. Everyone was intensely result-oriented in a spirit of cooperation, harmony, and synergy.

4. Leadership of the action. The fourth quality of the top teams was that the leader "led the action." The leader of the team was not only a peer and a friend, but he actively worked to achieve the goals of the team. He set an example and was a role model for the others.

The top leaders in the best teams saw themselves more as "blockers" rather than as commanders or directors. As blockers, they defined one of their main jobs as the removal of any obstacles that might be holding one of the team members back from doing the very best job possible. They concerned themselves with small things like air conditioning, comfortable furniture, computer screens, transportation, and other resources. The leader viewed his job as helping the other team players to do their jobs.

5. Continuous evaluation of results. The best teams continually assessed and evaluated their progress and results. They asked at their staff meetings, "How are we doing? Is there anything we need to change? Is there anything we need to improve? Are our values, goals, and plans working well together?"

Externally, the top teams were always asking for feedback from their customers and other stakeholders. If they were doing something wrong, or if there was a defect in their work or their products, they wanted to know about it immediately so they could make changes. They were not afraid of criticism or complaints. In fact, they encouraged and welcomed negative feedback and used it as a springboard to be even better next time.

One of the characteristics of top teams, in every area of endeavor, is open communication. Conflict resolution is invariably accomplished by means of openness, honesty, and straight talk. There are no hurt feelings, resentments, or avoidance of difficult issues. Everything is laid on the table on a regular basis.

Three Keys to Assembling a Top Team

There are countless books and articles on building effective teams. You can reduce most of their recommendations down to three basic points: First, select the right people. Second, train them thoroughly. Third, manage them professionally.

Most of the success of your team will be determined by the people you select to be on the team in the first place. Since some of the people you select will not work out over time, and others will be only average performers, there is always the likelihood that one or more team members should not be there. If this is the case, ask the zero-based-thinking question, "If I had not hired this person, knowing what I now know, would I hire this person today?" If the answer is *no*, then your next question is, "How do I get rid of this person, and how fast?"

The rule is "Hire in haste, repent at leisure." Take your time in selecting your team members. As Harvey MacKay says, "Hire slow and fire fast." The quality of the people you select to work with you will determine your success in business more than any other factor.

Second, train your people thoroughly. It is absolutely amazing how many managers spend an enormous amount of money hiring and paying people and then neglect to train them. Here is the rule: You cannot expect a person to do a job properly unless you have thoroughly trained him to do that job.

Sometimes an employee may be only one skill away from being an outstanding contributor to your company. Most people are reluctant to admit that they are not good at something. Your ability to identify the needs of your staff for additional training and development in a particular area is a critical part of leadership.

Third, manage your staff professionally. The key to success in business is summarized in the phrase "hands-on management." The best managers spend 75 percent of their time or more interacting with their staff. They are constantly moving around. They are meeting, greeting, talking to them in hallways, discussing problems with them in meetings, having lunch or coffee with them, and continually keeping the channels of communication open.

Good managers are fully engaged in the process of management. They are fully aware that their job is to make sure that everyone else is positive, confident, and prepared to do *their* jobs. A good manager at work is like a parent at home. A parent at home has children for whom he is responsible. The manager at work has employees for whom she is responsible. They are often just like children, but with better excuses.

Today, most employees are knowledge workers. Knowledge workers are very different from manual workers. Knowledge workers insist upon being treated in a friendly way, as peers. They want to be respected for their particular expertise and valued for their contribution. This is a key responsibility of management.

Afghanistan

The war in Afghanistan that began in 2001 is a brilliant example of concerted action. Commander-in-Chief of the U.S. Central Command Tommy Franks of the Southern Command of the U.S. Army, in coordination with the soldiers and officers of the navy, the air force, and the marines, directed and coordinated every element of the campaign. Everyone at every level knew exactly what was expected of them and when and where.

The coordination between the forces on the ground and the supporting airpower was so devastating that the Taliban forces, which had defeated the Russian army in ten years of warfare, was effectively neutralized within six weeks. Concerted action is a powerful tool and an absolute prerequisite for achieving military victory.

Empowerment Made Simple

The word "empower" means to "put power into." When you empower your staff by encouraging and motivating them, they become more powerful in achieving the results that you need from them. Excellent managers are continually seeking ways to make people feel better about themselves. They constantly praise, encourage, and reward positive behaviors. They build self-esteem and self-confidence by "catching people when they are doing something right."

Many thousands of employees have been interviewed and asked about the qualities of the best managers they have ever worked for. It turns out that the best managers practice the four C's in their interactions with their staff.

The first "C" is *Clarity*. It turns out that the greatest motivator in the world of work is knowing exactly what is expected. The greatest demotivator, on the other hand, is not knowing what is expected. The best managers take the time to be absolutely clear with each employee about what that employee is expected to do, and in what order of priority, and to what standard of performance. Everybody knows and understands their job. This is a real key to empowerment.

The second "C" stands for *Consideration*. Employees described their best managers with the words, "I always felt he considered me as a person as well as an employee."

The best managers take the time to show consideration and concern for the personal lives of their employees. They listen patiently when their employees want to talk. They commiserate with them when they have problems. They ask about their families, and they recognize their birthdays. They treat their employees as special and important people.

In my company, fully half of my employees, men and women, have young children. So do I. Early on, I recognized the stress that a person can experience if their child has a problem or need of any kind. I therefore instituted a policy called "children come first."

Under this policy, any of my employees can leave at any time if one of their children requires their presence. No time or pay is deducted. If, for some reason, their child requires their attention, and they cannot come into work, we find a way to work around it. But "children come first."

How has this policy worked? In ten years, the policy has never been abused. When you treat people as responsible, intelligent adults, they act like responsible, intelligent adults. The best part of all is that none of my staff feel any stress or pressure about their children because "children come first." And surprise, surprise! The job always gets done. This is a policy that I would heartily recommend to any business or organization. What it does for morale is absolutely wonderful.

The third "C" stands for *Caring*. Excellent managers genuinely care about the members of their staff. And each person feels this sense of caring by the company and by the manager. When people feel cared for by their superiors, they are empowered to give of their very best.

Caring is a wonderful way to build loyalty and commitment among your people. As they say, "They don't care how much you know until they know how much you care." This is very true.

The fourth "C" stands for *Courtesy*. One of the best ways to approach employees and team members today is to treat them as if they were *volunteers*. Imagine that they have given up their time voluntarily to come to work for you at no pay. If you think of them as volunteers, working for you out of the goodness of their hearts, without pay, you will treat them very differently than the old-school way of "Do it my way or hit the highway."

The practice of courtesy requires that you speak politely and respectfully to each person. You treat them at all times as if they were important customers of your business. You say "Thank you" for everything they do for you.

Perhaps the best management principle of all is what I call "Golden Rule Management." Treat every person who works for you exactly as you would want them to treat you if you were working for them. It often happens in our turbulent economy that a person who is a manager today finds himself or herself working for a subordinate a couple of years from now. Be sure to treat everybody who works for you today as if you might be working for them at a future time. This will keep you on your best behavior.

Be a Good Team Player

General Dwight D. Eisenhower, Supreme Allied Commander in World War II, was the embodiment of a great team player. Using the skills of diplomacy, combined with tremendous patience and backed with iron resolve, he was able to bring together the leaders of different armies and weld them into an overwhelmingly effective fighting force. Without losing sight of his objective, to liberate Europe, he was able to balance and compromise conflicting interests to unite everyone in pursuit of a common goal.

Rudyard Kipling wrote, "The strength of the wolf is the pack, and the strength of the pack is the wolf." The team is only as good as the individual team members. One of the most important qualities of a good team player is that she is totally *committed* to the success of the team and of the organization. In other words, she is committed to winning, to victory for her group.

Your goal is to be totally committed to victory. Everybody is watching and everybody notices. Everyone knows who makes the greatest contribution and who does only the bare minimum.

Napoleon Hill once wrote that "No one can ever stop you from going the extra mile at work." Always look for ways to make a greater contribution, to put in more than anyone else. In staff meetings, always volunteer for assignments. Keep looking for opportunities to do more than anyone else. Continue raising your hand when something needs to be done. The important people are watching and noticing.

The very best team players are those who volunteer for assignments and then get the job done quickly and well. Getting a reputation as a hard worker who does the job quickly will open more doors for you than you can possibly imagine.

There is an old Chinese saying, "He who would rule must learn to obey." The most successful people in business today were outstanding team members and employees in their younger years. As a result, they were continually paid more and promoted faster, over the heads of the average employee who just does what he has to do to avoid being fired or laid off.

Motivating People to Peak Performance

There are three keys to motivation that you can practice with all the people who report to you. They are Recognition, Rewards, and Reinforcement. Practice all three of them with as many people as possible, as often as you can.

Most people are starved for recognition, especially recognition that comes from the important people in their lives. In fact, the more important you are in the eyes of another person, the more powerful and influential are your statements to that person. As a manager or leader, you are in a wonderful position to have an incredible impact on the people who report to you.

Praise and recognize people for little accomplishments as well as large accomplishments. Find reasons to compliment them for their work or their achievements. Smile when you see them, and treat them with respect and esteem. Recognition is a powerful motivator for people at all ages and in all situations.

Rewards are a vital part of motivating people to peak performance. The primary reward that people want is more money. In study after study, employees repeat, over and over, that what they really want for excellent performance is financial rewards. People also like awards, prizes, trips, plaques, and trophies. But most of all, people want more money.

It is often better to give small cash prizes for outstanding performance rather than salary increases. The first is fixed and limited while the other one goes on indefinitely. But continually look for ways to reward people for doing an excellent job. Remember the greatest management principle in the world articulated by Michael LeBoeuf, "What gets rewarded gets done."

The third key to motivation is reinforcement. "What gets reinforced gets repeated." Whenever you talk about, praise, and comment on a particular behavior, the individual will be more likely to repeat that behavior in the future. The flipside of motivation is that if you do not recognize, reward, and reinforce a particular behavior, the individual may simply stop doing it.

If a person who is habitually late to work starts making an effort to come in on time, you should praise and recognize her punctuality each time it occurs until it becomes a new habit. When people come to meetings on time, you should thank them and praise them for being punctual.

Look for every opportunity to give recognition, rewards, and reinforcement for the behaviors that you want to see repeated by that individual and by other people in the company.

The Principle of Concerted Action and Personal Success

Much of your happiness in life will be determined by your relationships with other people. Unfortunately, most of your problems and aggravations in life will also be the result of problems and difficulties with other people. You therefore owe it to yourself to become excellent at relationship management and at working well with others.

Everything you do in life involves other people. The very best families are models of concerted action. They work together harmoniously, sharing the work and the responsibilities and genuinely enjoying each other's company.

Unhappy families and groups are those where there is continual criticism, complaining, backbiting, and friction. People make little effort to get along and are continually picking away at each other. One of your most important goals is to practice the principle of concerted action in your personal relationships. This is the key to happiness and well-being.

Make a list of all the important people in your family and in your social life. Determine what it is that they want or need from you in order to be happy in their relationships with you.

What are your goals for your relationships with the key people in your life? Especially with regard to your family, what is it you want to accomplish in your family life? What do you want to do with or for the key people in your life?

Balance Between Work and Family

To be happy, you need to establish a healthy balance between your work and your family life. You achieve this by setting balance as a priority and then by making the changes necessary for putting your life back into better balance.

There are only four ways in which you can change your life. You can do *more* of some things or you can do *less* of other things. You can *start* doing something that you are not doing today or you can *stop* doing something altogether.

To get your life back into balance, sit down with the members of your family, and ask them four questions: "Is there anything that I am doing that you would like me to do *more* of? Is there anything that I am doing that you would like me to do *less* of? Is there anything that I am not doing that you would like me to *start* doing? Is there anything that I am doing that you would like me to *stop* doing altogether?"

If you have the courage to ask these questions, you had better bring a lunch because you are going to be there for a long time listening to the answers.

There is a simple two-part formula for achieving and maintaining balance between your work and family life. This formula requires that you divide your life into these two basic parts. You then develop a strategy for each part.

At work, discipline yourself to "work all the time you work." Don't fool around or waste time. Don't chat with co-workers, make personal phone calls, read the newspaper, take long lunches, or go shopping. Work all the time you work! Remember, if you don't get your work done, it doesn't go away. You have to take it home. As a result, when you waste time at work, you rob your family of your personal time. This is not a good policy.

The second part of the formula has to do with your family. When you are with your family, be there 100 percent of the time. Remember, the only time that you are really *with* another person is when you are "in their face." It is only when you are head-to-head, and knee-to-knee.

Resolve to spend at least one hour per day with your spouse and at least ten to twenty minutes each day with each of your children. You can spend more if you like but it is not a good idea to spend less.

The rule for balance is this: "It is *quality* of time at work that counts and *quantity* of time at home."

Work requires *quality* time. Quality time is when you work fully focused on the highest value use of your time. You get on with the job and get it done quickly. You set priorities and work on your top tasks most of the time. You focus and concentrate on results throughout the workday. When you work, you work!

Relationships on the other hand, require *quantity* time. Relationships require long, unbroken periods of unstructured time to be truly enjoyable. "We live life by the years but we only experience it in the *moments*." The most precious moments in your personal relationships come unexpectedly and unbidden. And they only come when you create large blocks of relaxed time that allow those wonderful moments to occur.

The Principle of Concerted Action Revisited

No one does it alone. Everything you accomplish in life requires the active cooperation of other people. The more capable you are of getting along with other people, the happier and more successful you will be, both at work and at home.

Truly excellent men and women have developed a wonderful ability to get along well with a great number of other different people. They have high levels of self-confidence and self-esteem. They like and respect themselves, and as a result, they like and respect others. They work in harmony with others toward common and mutually agreed-upon goals.

They are excellent team players. They focus on contribution. They are considered to be among the most valuable people in their companies and in their social circles.

Practice the principle of concerted action in everything you do. When you develop a large network of harmonious relationships, you are then able to multiply yourself and your abilities times all the people you know and who know you. You become unstoppable.

The Principle of Unity of Command

One Person in Charge

Nothing is so important in war as an undivided command: for this reason, when war is carried on against a single power, there should be only one army, acting upon one base, and conducted by one chief.

—NAPOLEON

The key to success in business or warfare is singleness of vision, complete clarity with one set of instructions, and one person in charge making the strategic decisions. A confusion of visions leads to misunderstandings, ineffectiveness, and defeat in warfare and in business.

The Battle of Gettysburg

Robert E. Lee was one of the finest fighting generals ever produced by the U.S. Army. Throughout the Civil War, he achieved

141

a series of brilliant victories against superior forces. In virtually every attack or defense, the Union army outnumbered him. The greatest battle of his career, and the decisive battle of the war, took place at Gettysburg on July 1–3, 1863. Lee's failure to impose unity of command on his officers prior to and during this battle led to his defeat at Gettysburg and the eventual downfall of the Confederacy.

First, instead of instructing General Jeb Stuart and his cavalry to stay close to his army and continually reconnoiter the terrain, he let Stuart go off on a long, roundabout ride that only brought him and his cavalry to Gettysburg on the second day of the battle. By that time, it was too late. Lee had blundered unprepared into the entire Union army at Gettysburg because of his lack of adequate intelligence, which Stuart was supposed to have provided.

The forces of Robert E. Lee and the Army of Northern Virginia might still have won the Battle of Gettysburg if it had not been for another incident of divided command. Military historians generally agree that the failure of General James Longstreet to move forward early on the second day of the battle was the critical action (or non-action) that led to the Confederate defeat.

Lee had instructed Longstreet to move the divisions under his command forward on the right flank and seize the hill called Little Round Top at the end of Cemetery Ridge on the Union's extreme left flank. But Longstreet was not happy with this order. He felt that it would be better to attempt a wide flanking maneuver around the Union left flank and attack them from behind. As a result, he held his forces back for most of the second day. When he finally ordered them forward, Union forces under the command of Colonel Joshua Chamberlain had recognized the danger and had rushed troops to secure Little Round Top. The failure to take Little Round Top in the battle that followed arguably led to the defeat of the Confederate Army at Gettysburg the following day.

In all areas of life, a single vision, a single leader, a single commander or executive must make the critical strategic decisions that determine the success of the battle or the organization. Anything other than unity of command leads to confusion, uncertainty, diffusion of effort, and, ultimately, defeat.

> **THE PRINCIPLE OF UNITY OF COMMAND:**
> For every objective, there should be unity of effort
> under one responsible commander.

Unity of effort requires that all elements of a force work harmoniously toward a common goal, and it implies the development of coordination of the full combat powers of the available forces. Cooperation further contributes to unity of effort, but only when a single individual is responsible for the activities of a group can the group operate at its peak efficiency in its quest to achieve an assigned goal. Coalition warfare creates a challenge for the principle of unity of command because of the unwillingness of groups to place their resources under the control of a commander from one of the other groups in the coalition.

The Principle of Unity of Command in Business

In every organization, whether collegial, participatory, democratic, hierarchical, or any other kind of management system, there has to be a single person in charge of achieving each goal and at each point of responsibility. There has to be a place where, as President Harry Truman said, "The buck stops here."

When Lee Iacocca took over Chrysler Corporation in 1979, the company was on the verge of bankruptcy. The first thing he found upon arriving was that there were thirty-six vice presidents of Chrysler Corporation worldwide, each of whom had his own fiefdom. Each of them was in competition with the other vice presidents. There was no clear leadership. If someone did not agree with a senior management decision, they simply delayed and dragged their feet on the decision and eventually assured that nothing got done.

Iacocca immediately took command. He reorganized the corporation, fired thirty-five of the thirty-six vice presidents, went to Congress to get a loan guarantee, renegotiated Chrysler's loans with more than 400 banks, renegotiated contracts with 350,000 Chrysler workers, and renegotiated prices with 4,000 suppliers. Within four years, he had turned the company around, paid back the loans in full, and generated 350 million dollars in profits. Lee Iacocca will always be remembered for this feat as one of the great business leaders of the twentieth century.

When IBM ran into serious trouble in 1991 and 1992, Lou Gerstner was brought from RJR Nabisco as the new president. He immediately took command. He reorganized the company and its divisions to make them more competitive. He consolidated some divisions with others and discontinued product and service areas that were no longer profitable. Within two years, he had turned IBM around, from losses to profits, and put the company back on the map. Under his leadership, the IBM stock price increased more than 700 percent!

Jack Welch, arguably the finest chief executive of the twentieth century, led General Electric to forty-eight consecutive quarters of increased profits. He turned an $800-million-dollar-a-year company into a $50-billion-dollar international giant. He projected his vision with his leadership maxims, such as, "If we don't have competitive advantage, we won't compete" and "We will be either number one or number two in every market segment, or we will get out of that business."

In every case, successful business leaders are those who accurately assess the needs of the situation, make clear decisions, and then take vigorous action. Leaders form a clear idea of what needs to be done. They then have the ability to communicate this vision to everyone whose help will be required to fulfill it. They motivate everyone around them to work toward common goals. Unity of command, based on clear objectives, offensive action, concentration of powers, the ability to maneuver, excellent intelligence and knowledge of the market situation—all lead to concerted action and business victory.

Lead from the Front

General Norman Schwarzkopf, the American and allied commander in the Gulf War, tells about one of the most important pieces of advice he ever received as an officer. When he was promoted to a command at the Pentagon, he asked his senior officer how he should handle the enormous complexities of the position. His senior officer said these words: "When placed in command, take charge!" This is the guiding principle of men and women who rise to positions of power and influence within their organization: "Take charge!"

In the Bible a master says, "Oh good and faithful servant, you have been master over small things, I will make you master over large things." In business, this means that when you accept responsibility and take charge in smaller things, you will be given larger and larger responsibilities to carry out. Your performance of today determines your opportunities of tomorrow.

The Seven Responsibilities of Leadership

The two requirements for an excellent leader are character and competence. Character refers to your personal qualities of integrity, courage, and persistence. Your competence is measured by how capable you are of leading, managing, and getting the job done. This is vital to your creating a high degree of unity and commitment among the people who report to you.

There are seven critical areas where you must perform consistently well to become an excellent executive and fulfill your responsibilities to yourself and your organization.

Job number one: Set and achieve business goals. This is the first area where clarity is essential. You must know exactly what it is you are trying to accomplish and how you will measure success when you achieve it.

In a recent *Fortune* article investigating the reasons why twenty-eight CEOs of Fortune 500 companies had been fired in the previous three years, one fault stood out above all others: "Failure to execute."

In warfare, a military commander is given the responsibility of achieving victory against the enemy. In business, each executive at every level is given the responsibility to achieve specific, measurable business victories or *goals*. The inability to get the required results, and to achieve the goals in a timely fashion, is the primary reason for failure, frustration, and firing at every level, in every company, large or small.

Take the time to develop absolute *clarity* about what it is you expect to accomplish to justify your position and earn your pay. Then focus and concentrate all your energies on achieving that goal, or goals, in a timely fashion. Your reputation for achieving essential goals will help you more than anything else you can do.

When General George C. Marshall, chief of staff of the U.S. Army during World War II, was urged to replace the arrogant and outspoken General George S. Patton, he told his critics, "I can't spare this man; he wins battles."

Job number two: Innovate and market. Cash flow is the "blood to the brain" of every business organization. Cash flow comes from the ability to generate sales and revenues in a timely fashion. Sales generation requires continuous innovation and an un-relenting focus on marketing and selling the products and services of the company.

Apply the "CANEI Strategy" to your sales and marketing efforts. *CANEI* stands for "Continuous and Never-Ending Improvement." Never be satisfied. Look for new, better, faster, and cheaper ways to market and sell your products, every day, and every hour of the day.

Victory in business terms means the ability to win customers, to capture markets, and to generate sales and revenues in excess of their costs. The ability of the executive or entrepreneur to innovate and market continuously is the ultimate determinant of business success, profitability, and promotion.

Job number three: Solve problems and make decisions. Whatever title appears on your business card can be crossed out and replaced with the words "*Problem-Solver.*" This is your *real* job. You solve problems from morning to night. Your success is largely determined by how effective you are at solving the problems that arise in your work.

Effective executives are good at solving problems. They make the *right* decisions, and they make their decisions *right*.

Whenever you are faced with a difficulty at work, ask, "What exactly is the problem?" Beware of a problem for which there is only one definition. Restate the problem in several different ways to make it more amenable to a solution. Always ask, "What *else* is the problem?"

In solving problems, think and talk exclusively in terms of *solutions*. Focus all your attention on the specific actions you can take to solve the problem. Whatever the situation, make the necessary decisions, and continue moving forward. Forget about the past and who is to blame. Focus on the future and what actions you can take now. Take command.

Job number four: Set priorities, and work on key tasks.
One of your key responsibilities is to be working on your most vital task all the time and to assure that everyone who reports to you is also working on their key tasks.

Remember that only 20 percent of what you do accounts for 80 percent of your results. According to Robert Half International, fully 50 percent of time at work is wasted doing things that contribute nothing to the goals of the company. Of the 50 percent of time that is actually spent on the work, much of that is wasted as well on low-value tasks.

Always ask yourself, "What are my highest value activities?" If you could only do one thing all day long, what one task would that be?

Your ability to set correct priorities on the expenditure of time and resources is an essential skill of leadership. The very worst use of time is to do efficiently what need not be done at all.

Job number five: Concentrate single-mindedly on the one activity that can make the greatest difference. Long-term potential consequences are the key to setting priorities. Always ask yourself, "What is likely to happen if I complete, or fail to complete this particular task?" Something that is very important is something for which there are serious consequences, one way or the other.

Write down everything you have to do before you begin. Set priorities on your list by using the ABCDE system. An "A" task is something that is very important. It has serious consequences. A "B" task is something that should be done but has only minor consequences. A "C" task is something that it would be nice to do but that has no consequences at all, like going out for lunch or reading the newspaper.

A "D" task is something that you can delegate to other people. You should use your creativity to delegate everything you possibly can to free up more time for the few tasks that only you can do.

An "E" task is something that you can eliminate altogether. It may have been important at one time, but it does not contribute to the achievement of your goals today.

You can only get your time and your life under control to the degree to which you *stop* doing certain things. Practice "creative abandonment" with tasks that no longer contribute to accomplishing your most important goals.

Job number six: Perform and get results. This is how you are judged every single day. Your ability to get results determines your pay, your promotion, your success, and the respect and esteem in which you are held by the people around you.

Identify your key result areas, the tasks that you absolutely, positively have to do well in order to be successful. Set standards of performance on each of those tasks. Be sure that you can *measure* whether or not you have done the job in an excellent fashion.

Determine your critical success factors, those key metrics that tell you what is happening in each important area. Focus and concentrate on these critical numbers. Continually work to improve them.

Ask yourself continually, "What results are expected of me?" Whatever your answer to this question, work on these specific results single-mindedly. They are the major determinants of your success.

Job number seven: Be a role model for others. This is something only you can do, and it is perhaps the most important responsibility of leadership. One of the marks of superior executives is that they conduct themselves as though everyone were watching them even when no one is watching. Top people set higher standards for themselves than others would set for them.

Immanuel Kant, the German philosopher, postulated his universal maxim more than 200 years ago. He said, "Live your life as though your every act were to become universal law for all people."

The highest achievement for a leader is the development of "moral excellence." On this plane of behavior, the leader practices the highest virtues of courage, integrity, and character that it is possible for a person to have. The leader holds his *own* feet to the fire. He continually raises the bar on himself. He never makes excuses for his performance. He refuses to blame problems or difficulties on his subordinates. The leader acts as if everyone in the organization were looking to him to set the example for how they were supposed to behave. For example, Alexander the Great, even after he had conquered the greatest empire in the ancient world, always led his armies into battle personally. He rode at the front of his men to demonstrate to them that he had complete confidence in the outcome of the battle. He showed no fear. As a result, his soldiers were eager to follow throughout his brief but glorious career. (He died of pneumonia at the age of 32). Another example is General Patton. Patton was famous for going forward to the battlefront where he could observe what was taking place at first hand. His soldiers were amazed to see their general at the front, sharing the same dangers that they were facing. Stories of Patton's courage under fire spread throughout the Third Army and greatly encouraged his men. General Norman Schwarzkopf was an infantry commander in Vietnam and was wounded on two occasions. He demonstrated to his men that he was willing to go forward in the face of danger. This boosted morale among his troops and contributed to his success in the Gulf War.

Perhaps nothing contributes more to unity of command than for subordinates to work under someone they greatly respect and admire. Your commitment to becoming a great person, and to demonstrating your values in your every act, is perhaps the most important quality of leadership.

The Iranian Hostage Rescue Attempt

Unity of command is essential for maximum effectiveness. During the Iranian hostage crisis of 1979–1980, President Jimmy

Carter decided to launch a military operation to free the hostages held in the American Embassy in Tehran. But instead of putting a competent general in command of the entire operation, the command duties were split among heads of the U.S. Army, Navy, Air Force, Marines, and even a contingent from the Coast Guard. For political reasons, each arm of the U.S. military wanted to be involved and acquire some of the glory that would be attached to the expected success.

As if the divided command on the ground were not bad enough, President Carter and his Pentagon chiefs continually gave orders and counter-orders from Washington by satellite to the forces on the ground in Iran. This lack of unity of command doomed the mission to failure. Contingents were separated from each other. Essential spare parts and fuel were lacking. No one was quite sure who to report to or who was in charge. The proposed Iranian hostage rescue was a military debacle and contributed substantially to the loss of the presidency by Jimmy Carter in 1980.

Crisis Is Inevitable

In studies done at Stanford University on the career path of those who become chief executive officers of Fortune 500 corporations, the researchers discovered that "The ability to function effectively in a crisis" was the most important single quality of great business leadership.

However, they made an important observation with regard to crisis management. They found that the ability to deal with a crisis could not be taught in a classroom or with case studies. It was only in an actual crisis that a person demonstrated whether or not she was capable of handling a crisis at all.

Amidst the turbulence of today's business world, you will experience a business crisis of some kind every two or three months. By definition, a *crisis* comes completely unbidden and unanticipated. Like a Mack truck coming out of an alley, it hits you with no warning or opportunity for you to prepare. And it is at this moment that you demonstrate the quality of your character.

"The only inevitable event in the life of the leader is the recurring crisis."

—PETER DRUCKER

Epictetus, the Greek philosopher, wrote, "Circumstances do not make the man; they merely reveal him to himself." The very best leaders are those who are at their best when facing a situation of unexpected danger or reversal. It is only in crisis that you demonstrate your ability to remain calm and cool under fire.

In psychology, there is a powerful principle called "mental rehearsal." You can prepare for a crisis in advance by rehearsing how you will respond when the inevitable crisis occurs. You mentally prepare and you resolve that you will remain calm and in control, no matter what happens. Then, when the crisis arises, you will be ready to respond at your best.

Crisis Anticipation

The ability to anticipate what might happen in the future, and then to inform all concerned parties of the roles they will play should a certain event occur, is a critical part of achieving unity of command.

Royal Dutch Shell is famous for its commitment to "scenario planning." The company has invested millions of dollars and decades of time and research in thinking through and preparing for various scenarios that might occur to interrupt their worldwide business. By 2000, they had fully developed more than 620 scenarios covering every possibility from pipeline ruptures in the Arctic to coups d'état in oil-producing African nations. No matter what happens in the world of oil production and distribution, they have an alternate plan already prepared and ready to go.

One of the most important exercises you engage in while running your business and your life is to "play down the chessboard." Look into the future, six months, twelve months, and even three to five years. Make a list of the three to five worst things that could possibly happen in your personal and business life. What are they?

Imagine the loss of one or more of your major customers. Imagine your bank cutting off your credit. Imagine your product or service becoming obsolete or illegal. Imagine one or more of the key people in your business dying or leaving the company. What are the very worst things that could happen that could threaten the survivability of your business? What could you do to guard against them occurring?

Throughout history, until the 1800s, battles were directed by the general from his command post. Messengers and riders brought back information on the development of the battle, and the commander immediately made decisions to move or redeploy his forces. The ability to function well in the midst of a battle was essential for ultimate victory. Because of his place at the crossroads of information flows, the commander could assure that only one person was given the critical commands that determined the movements and actions of the different forces involved in the battle.

Napoleon was famous for reconnoitering the sites of his battles carefully before the first shot was fired. He had a finely developed sensitivity for the roll of the terrain and for the various features of the landscape that could be used to hide or move troops. He visualized how a battle might unfold, how his troops might move on the battlefield, and how his enemies might respond to the various movements he could make. By the time the battle began, Napoleon had thought through all the various scenarios that might unfold during the course of the conflict. This enabled him to be the single commander having a vision and understanding of the entire battlefield and what could be done to achieve victory. Because command was unified in one man, every divisional commander knew that his orders were a part of a larger plan of battle.

Napoleon was legendary for his quickness of decision when he was brought information on the shifting fortunes of his various detachments. What the people around him did not know was that he had carefully thought through every possibility well in advance. Whatever happened, he was prepared to instantly make a decision and take action. What appeared to be brilliance (which it was) was really evidence of careful advance mental preparation. You should do the same.

Whatever the worst possible events are that could occur sometime in your future, begin today to develop alternate scenarios. Determine the worst thing that could possibly go wrong, and then make sure that it doesn't happen. Follow the Boy Scout motto, "Be Prepared."

Power and Influence in Business

The more power and influence you have inside and outside of your organization, the more opportunities you will have, and the more successful you will be. The development of power and influence is an important personal strategy for you throughout your career.

Power in its simplest terms is the ability to influence, control, and direct the deployment of people and resources. A military commander can order large numbers of people to take specific actions, even sending them to their deaths. The leader of a large organization can tell large numbers of people what they must do to achieve the goals of the business. Political leaders, especially those who sit on Senate or Congressional committees, have the ability to direct and deploy huge financial resources. In each case, this gives these people extraordinary power.

People who have power over us have the ability to help us or to hurt us. We greatly respect, and even fear, people who can help us achieve our goals or hinder us in some way. We are inordinately influenced by those who we feel can have inordinate influence over us. One of your goals should be to develop this kind of power in your work.

When you start at your first job, you have little or no power at all. Your aim is to acquire some sort of power as quickly as possible. Your job is to become valuable, and then indispensable. Fortunately there are tried and proven ways to do this.

The first power that you can develop is called "expert power." This power comes from your ability to do your job in an excellent fashion. The better you are at doing a job that is important to your company, the more power and influence accrue to you. The more impact you can have on the sales or cash flow of a business, the more power and influence you have within that organization.

A study was conducted recently on the relative power and influence of managers and supervisors in a large brewery. Because of the nature of beer marketing, market share grows or declines very slowly. Therefore, the key to cash flow in a brewery is regular, predictable, consistent production and delivery of the product to the various commercial and retail outlets. Any interruption in the flow of the product immediately causes beer consumers to buy another brand. The revenues from those lost cannot be recouped, and sometimes the customer can be lost permanently. The continuous production of the beer is therefore the key to cash flow and company survival.

Therefore, it was not the president, vice president, controller, vice president of marketing, or anyone else who had the most power within a brewery operation. It turned out to be the chief engineer, the man in charge of the machinery and equipment, the continuous production process. The chief engineer was the person who ultimately determined if the brewery would remain in continuous operation. As a result, he was the most powerful person in the company and had the greatest influence in management circles.

Look at your own business. Who is the most indispensable single person in terms of continuous cash flow? How important are *you* to continuous cash flow? If you were to leave for a month, what would happen to the fortunes of your business?

The people with the greatest power and influence are those whose departure would cause the greatest immediate disruption in sales and cash flow. One of the ways that you develop greater power in your organization is by working your way into a position where you are vital to the revenues of the business.

If you are already in such a position, how can you increase your influence over those revenues? If you are not, how could you make yourself indispensable to continuing operations?

Remember the story of the salesman who accounted for fully 40 percent of the sales revenue of the company. In actuality, he was more important than the president or the vice president because of his "expert power."

The second form of power that you need to develop on your way up is called "referent power" or "ascribed power." This refers to the power and influence that you develop because of your personality. When you are optimistic, cheerful, and well-liked by your boss and co-workers, they will support you and want you to have a more prominent position in the organization.

People are promoted most rapidly when the people above them, below them, and on both sides of them want them to be promoted. The more people *like* you, the more they will go out of their way to help you and cooperate with you to make you more successful in your company.

You develop *ascribed power* by continually looking for ways to help other people to do their jobs. You volunteer for assignments, and you step forward when someone needs something done. You go out of your way to do little things for other people, even when they cannot help you, or when there are no direct rewards. Every day, you practice the Dale Carnegie rule: "Make friends and influence people." By the Law of Sowing and Reaping, the more you put in, the more you will eventually get out. People around you will help far more than they would help someone who does not make the extra effort.

The third form of power that you eventually attract is called "position power." This power accrues to a position or title. It gives you the right to reward and punish, to give instructions to other people, to spend money, and to allocate other resources. Position power is the highest form of power. A new person, brought in from the outside and given an important title, immediately assumes all the power and influence that goes along with that title. One of your career goals is to achieve the highest and most influential position that is possible for you.

Each of these forms of power occurs in sequence. As you develop a reputation for doing a great job, the important people around you will want to see you given more responsibilities and opportunities. You will be paid more and promoted faster. When you treat other people well, they will want to help you to be more successful. Soon you will be give *position power* and the rewards that go along with it.

Hierarchy Is Essential

In every large organization, including and especially in a military organization, there is a clearly defined chain of command, from the top to the bottom. This chain of command is essential to assure cohesion, coordination, and cooperation at every level in the achievement of military objectives.

Edmond O. Wilson, the Harvard biologist, writer of many books and articles on the human condition says, "The first law of human nature is hierarchy." He explains that all human beings absolutely need to know where they fit within the hierarchy of other human beings. This is why each person should have only one boss. Each person needs to know exactly where she stands in relation to every other person in the organization, and being responsible to one boss makes this clear.

Each person has to be answerable to only one person. Each person has to know who is above and who is below him. People can only perform at their best when they fully understand the hierarchy in their workplace. One of your responsibilities is to make this hierarchy absolutely clear and to remove any confusion or ambiguities about the chain of command.

In social situations, one of the first things we do upon meeting a new person is to find out where they are located in the social and economic hierarchy. In subtle ways, we try to find out what they do, how much they earn, what standard of living they enjoy, what sort of activities they engage in, where they went to school, what kind of background they have, and numerous other factors that enable us to pinpoint their location relative to us in our societal hierarchy.

In a smoothly functioning business, with a unified command structure, there is a direct line from the top person down to the bottom. Even in a collegial environment, where everyone functions as friends and peers, there still must be a single person who has the power and the authority to make the final decisions. Any failure to establish this framework and hierarchy will eventually lead to political machinations, misunderstandings, hurt feelings, anger, and even to the loss of valuable staff members.

The Principle of Unity of Command in Personal Life

You want to get the very most out of yourself and to live a wonderful life. To do this, you must impose a unity of command over your own life as well as that of your work.

Unity of command in personal life means that you take the time to think through who you really are and what you really want. You organize your values in a hierarchy, deciding what is more important to you and what is less important to you.

You analyze the various aspects of your life—your career, your family, your finances, your health, and your personal interests—and then determine what is more important to you and what is less important.

You decide upon your goals in each area of your life and determine your most important goal, your major definite purpose. You then make detailed plans of action and organize your actions by priority. Every day, you focus on doing more of the tasks that contribute the most to accomplishing your most important goals. You allocate your time carefully to assure that you are spending more time on those activities that contribute the very most to your highest values and priorities in life.

Take some time each day to think about your life and your work. Stand back and ask yourself, "If I were not doing what I am doing today, knowing what I now know, would I start it up again today?"

The Battle of Cannae

In the Second Punic War (218–201 B.C.), the Carthaginian general Hannibal crossed the Alps into Italy, losing half his infantry and one third of his cavalry. He arrived in the Po Valley in northern Italy with about 20,000 infantry, 6,000 cavalry, and only a few remaining war elephants. With the masterful use of cunning, deception, and speed, Hannibal destroyed three Roman armies sent against him, moving ever deeper into Italy, devastating the land and terrifying the Roman populace.

To counter the Carthaginian threat, the Roman Senate in 217 appointed Quintus Fabius Maximus as dictator for six months. He immediately adopted a course of action called the "Fabian Strategy." This was a policy of avoiding direct confrontation with Hannibal's armies and resorting to guerilla tactics instead.

When Fabius's six-month appointment ended, the Roman Senate, under political pressure to deal more aggressively with Hannibal, named two consuls, Terentius Varro and Aemilius Paullus, to head the army. They were ordered to attack and destroy Hannibal and his legions.

The senate made a fatal mistake. For political and personal reasons, they alternated the leadership of the army between the two consuls so that one would be in command every other day.

This was a classic example of divided command. The consequences for Rome were disastrous. Terentius Varro was arrogant and impetuous. Aemilius Paullus was cautious and careful. Hannibal's spies kept him informed of who was in charge of the Roman army each day, so he knew when to strike.

On August 2 in 216 B.C., Hannibal lined up his 47,000 infantry and cavalry on the west side of the Aufidus River, across the chord of an east-arching riverbed, thereby securing his flanks against the stream banks.

The Roman Army, 76,000 men strong, was encamped opposite the Carthaginians. Although Aemilius Paullus was reluctant, he realized he could no longer avoid giving battle to Hannibal. At sunrise, Hannibal sent his skirmishing forces into the Roman camp rousing them from sleep. They were immediately ordered to form up in ranks, giving them no chance to eat or prepare. They were then marched into battle against the Carthaginians who had slept the night before and eaten well before the battle.

Varro now took command and ordered his legions to attack directly into the front of the outnumbered Carthaginian infantry. As the Romans pushed forward, the Carthaginians withdrew slowly, gradually forming a concave line, sagging inward more and more as the Roman Legionaries pressed them back.

Hannibal had placed his heavy cavalry and veteran African infantry on the left and right flanks, where they held firm. Soon the Romans had been lured into a deep bowl. On Hannibal's signal, the infantry on either flank closed to encircle the Roman army in a classic double envelopment strategy. The Carthaginians gradually tightened the circle around the Romans. They were trapped and unable to break out. According to the Roman historian Polybius, of 80,000 Roman infantry and 9,600 Roman cavalry who began the battle, 70,000 infantry and 9,230 cavalry were killed. Hannibal's losses were less than 6,000 men.

The two consuls were put in charge of the army with the belief that their differing personalities would balance each other. But instead of cooperating, they constantly competed with each other. It was this competition that Hannibal was able to exploit in luring the Roman Army into giving battle. This was a classic example of the importance of unity of command in a battle situation. The Carthaginians had it under Hannibal. The Romans lacked it under their two commanders. The result was a great victory for Carthage and the worst defeat for the Romans in the history of the Roman Empire.

Singleness of Purpose

Singleness of purpose is the key to success. It is only when you organize your life and activities around an overarching goal that you tap into your potential and release your powers for achievement. By selecting one goal that is more important than anything else, you unify your powers and bring all your energies to bear on the one objective, the attainment of which can make more of a difference in your life than anything else.

The Principle of Unity of Command Revisited

Unity of command is essential for the efficient functioning of a military unit, a business, and even a family. Everyone must know exactly who is in charge, who makes the decisions, and who is ultimately responsible.

In your personal life, you must live in harmony with your core values and your unifying principles, the qualities and virtues that you consider the most important in yourself and others. The more aligned you are with the good, the noble, and the true, the better a leader and the better a person you will be.

Be sure that what you are doing on the outside is in complete alignment with your true values and goals on the inside. Discipline yourself to make whatever decisions or sacrifices are necessary to live in harmony with your innermost convictions. Set high standards for yourself, and refuse to compromise them. Living in a way that is consistent with the very best you know eventually makes you unstoppable.

CHAPTER EIGHT

The Principle of Simplicity
Take the Direct Approach

Success in war depends upon the golden rule of war.
Speed—Simplicity—Boldness.

—GENERAL GEORGE S. PATTON

The ability of military commanders and business leaders to strip things down to their essentials and then to focus on the one or two actions that are indispensable for victory is the mark of a high order of intelligence.

Operation Market Garden

In September 1944, British Field Marshall Montgomery convinced General Dwight D. Eisenhower that he could bring World War II to a quick conclusion if he could just have enough men, matériel, and paratroopers to simultaneously

165

seize five key bridges over rivers and canals in the Netherlands and cross the Rhine River into Germany in force. At the same time, Allied tanks and infantry were to push through from the front line, relieve the airborne troops, and cross the bridges. Reluctantly, and because of political pressure from Churchill, Eisenhower allowed Montgomery to proceed with Operation Market Garden. This plan was in sharp contrast to Eisenhower's strategy of attacking along a broad Allied front, but he nonetheless allowed it to proceed. It turned out to be one of the big mistakes of the war.

In the midst of the planning for this operation, one of the intelligence officers, Lt. General Boy Browning, observed that, in attempting to take four bridges in a row, and then the fifth bridge at Arnhem, the allies were perhaps going "a bridge too far." This turned out to be exactly what happened.

In one of the most complex offensive operations of World War II, thousands of paratroopers were dropped throughout the Netherlands, each group assigned to seize a particular bridge near their drop area. However, because of faulty maps and poor information, many men were dropped miles from their assigned bridges. They then had to fight their way to the bridges over hotly contested terrain, armed only with light weapons.

The Allies received a warning that German troops were in the area, but the warning was late and was ignored. Some of the finest German infantry and Panzer Corps were refitting in the area. They were immediately put into action to counterattack the Allied troops landing all around them.

Meanwhile, there was only one road along which supplies for the beleaguered paratroopers could be brought. Maps turned out to be inaccurate, and entire regiments got lost.

There were communication problems as well as a lack of supplies and ammunition. Trucks broke down, and river crossing equipment went astray. More Allied troops were both dropped and trucked into the battle. There were not enough aircraft to deliver the troops all at once. The Germans also had anti-aircraft defenses near Arnhem that made it too dangerous for the gliders to land there; consequently, they landed seven miles away, thereby destroying the element of surprise. The Germans quickly figured out the Allied plan, reorganized their forces, and counterattacked fiercely. By the time Operation Market Garden collapsed, it had been a complete defeat, costing thousands of lives and leaving the Allies right back where they started. The entire offensive violated the principle of simplicity from the first moment.

The operation was ill conceived from the start. There were simply far too many variables, all of which had to come together at once to assure success. The complexity of the operation was such that virtually no one, at any level of command, had a clear idea of what was happening, or what could be done to minimize losses or achieve victory. In retrospect, it was a foolish waste of precious human and matériel resources.

THE PRINCIPLE OF SIMPLICITY:
Prepare clear, uncomplicated plans with clear, concise orders to assure thorough understanding.

In all communications, the commander should make every reasonable effort to eliminate the slightest chance of misunderstanding; simplicity contributes to this end. Simplicity does not imply that precise, detailed, and necessary information should be withheld from those who need such information to operate effectively.

The Principle of Simplicity in Business

Complexity and confusion are the worst enemies of successful business or military operations. There is a natural tendency toward complication and diffusion of effort in all human activities that must constantly be resisted. Einstein wrote, "Everything should be made as simple as possible, but no simpler." If you don't focus on simplicity, you get complexity by default.

The greater the simplicity with which you can execute your plans, the greater the power and force you can bring to bear on achieving your objectives. You must therefore be continually striving to find simpler and more efficient ways to accomplish every business task.

Occam's Razor

Around the year 1340, the English philosopher William of Occam proposed a decision-making tool that has helped to simplify and streamline thought for almost a thousand years. What he said was, "Entities should not be multiplied unnecessarily." Paraphrased for our day, this means, "In solving any problem, the simplest and most direct solution is usually the most correct solution." More than 1,700 years before Occam, Socrates taught that the most likely solution to any problem was probably the solution that had the fewest number of steps.

Whatever problem or difficulty you are dealing with, or whatever goal you are trying to achieve, ask yourself, "What is the simplest and most direct way of solving this problem or achieving this goal?" You may find that there is an obvious, easy way that will save you an enormous amount of time and money in achieving the same result.

Not long ago, I was working with a large organization that had set a goal of selling a million units of its new product during the first year of release. After eight hours of brainstorming among some of the brightest marketing people in the industry, the group came up with dozens of different ideas, all having varying degrees of complexity, by which a million units could be sold. I then proposed to them that they apply Occam's Razor to this question.

I said, "Rather than attempting to sell varying amounts of this new product through all of these different channels to all of these different customers, why don't you select a single large company or purchaser who can buy one million units in a single transaction?"

There was silence in the room. Some of them looked at me as if I was crazy. Then one of the executives spoke up and said, "I know a company for whom this product would be a perfect gift or bonus for every one of their customers, and they have several million customers." To make a long story short, they followed up on this idea and got a single order for one million units of the product. The goal was achieved.

The Law of Complexity

The natural tendency in all human activities is to increase the complexity of the procedure. But all progress in human activities, in science, technology, medicine, business, sales, marketing, and in every other area, comes from *simplifying* the process.

The first computer filled a warehouse and consumed as much electricity as a small town. Today, a handheld computer or PalmPilot has a hundred or a thousand times the computing power of that first Univac computer and is operated by a pair of AA batteries. The simplification of computing capability has been nothing short of miraculous in the last couple of decades.

Many surgeries used to require cutting open the human body, often scissoring through entire bone structures. Today, the most sophisticated surgeries can be conducted with small tubes inserted through tiny openings that leave imperceptible scars.

What used to take entire accounting departments with hundreds of people and tons of paper can now be done quickly and efficiently with small desktop computers. The movement toward simplification continues every day.

The Law of Complexity says, "In any process or procedure, the complexity of the activity increases by the square of the number of steps in that activity." This is my own personal discovery. But it proves to be true in virtually every field of human endeavor.

Complexity may be defined as "the *potential* for additional costs, mistakes, or time in the achievement of the goal." The more steps there are in any process, the more likely it is that the time to complete the process will increase, the cost of completing the process will go up, and the number of mistakes made in completing the process will multiply.

A job as simple as putting together a brochure or arranging an advertising campaign can have a complexity factor of five or ten. Most government activities have a complexity factor of ten or more. This means that the potential time required, the potential number of mistakes possible, and the potential cost of one of these complex tasks can be *outrageous*. This complexity factor explains how we get $700 hammers and $2,500 toilet seats in the Department of Defense. Every standard and regulation was followed, but because of the complexity involved, the costs were horrendous!

You must be continually alert to ways to reduce the number of steps in any process of work or goal achievement. Become extremely sensitive to any process that is complicated, knowing that the potential time, cost, and number of mistakes can be enormous. Simplify, simplify, simplify.

Simplifying Your Life

There are several things that you can do every day to simplify your business and your personal life. Any one of these actions can reduce the number of steps and increase the likelihood that you will achieve your goal faster and more cheaply than you might have thought possible.

1. Focus. The more time you take to develop absolute clarity about what you want and the very best way to achieve it, the faster and more easily you will accomplish that goal. Success is almost always the result of complete clarity.

Failure is almost always the result of fuzziness and confusion. There is a 90/10 rule that you can apply to improve your focus. This rule says that the first 10 percent of time that you take to think through the task or goal will save you 90 percent of the time and effort required to complete that task or accomplish that goal. Resolve to invest the necessary time in advance of beginning. This will save you an enormous amount of time repairing or redoing the task later.

2. Improve. Get better at your key tasks. The more knowledgeable and skilled you are at what you are doing, the faster and more easily you will get the job done. Hiring a skilled professional with years of experience at a particular job can be one of the smartest and cheapest things you do. Many companies have dramatically improved their results by adding one key person to their staff.

In your work life, identify the one task that, if you were to do it extremely well, would contribute the most to the quality and quantity of your results. Make the development of this skill a project or a goal. Write it down, make a plan, and work on getting a little better in that key area every single day. This decision alone can change your life.

3. Delegate. When you start off in your career, or when you start a new business, you have to do everything yourself. If you are not careful, you will develop the habit of doing things yourself. One of the main reasons for failure in a new job is the tendency to continue doing what you were doing before you were promoted.

These tasks and activities keep you in your comfort zone. Under the pressure of deadlines or when you have too much to do and too little time, you naturally fall back into your comfort zone and get busy doing the job yourself, rather than delegating it to others. This can really complicate your life.

However, delegation moves you from operating to managing. It takes you from what you can do personally to what you can control in the activities of others. Delegation is a key result area in management. It is an absolutely essential skill if you want to both reduce the complexity of your work and get more done at the same time.

Instead of thinking about how you can get the job done *personally*, think continually about how you can delegate it to someone else.

Make a habit of delegating everything you possibly can so that you can free up your time to do the few things that only you can do that can make a real difference to your company.

4. Outsource. Outsource every job and function in your business that can be done by another company that specializes in that area. Many companies outsource their payroll, their personnel, and their human resources administration. They outsource their hiring, their health care, their office maintenance, printing, mailing, advertising, and even travel.

If a particular department or function does not add sales, cash flow, or profits to your business, it is a perfect candidate for outsourcing. Another company that specializes in a particular service or activity can usually perform that function faster, better, and cheaper than you can while saving you the time and expense of doing it yourself.

5. Eliminate. In your home, you have cupboards full of things that you have accumulated over the years. For many reasons, many people develop a "pack rat" mentality. No matter how old or useless an item may be, they hold onto it "just in case."

In every business, there is an accumulation of tasks and activities that have gathered over the years. Many of them have no more value or use today. But they continue to take up time and space and cause expense. You must continually ask yourself, "What are they?" and "Why are we doing this?"

A new vice president of finance was hired into the accounting department of a Fortune 500 company. As he familiarized himself with the operations, he was introduced to a department with twelve full-time, highly paid employees. Their job was to assemble the worldwide sales results of the business each month into a large report that was then distributed throughout the company. This report was almost 300 pages thick and was usually completed by the end of the third week of the month and then sent out to all the key executives.

The following week, he was visiting one of the vice presidents who received this report each month. He asked him if he had received his copy of the report yet. The vice president assured him that he had. The vice president of finance asked him if he could see it. The other vice president took him down the hall to a filing cabinet, opened the filing cabinet, and there it was, along with the other reports.

"Do you read these reports?" he asked.

The vice president smiled sheepishly and said, "You know, I always mean to, but I am so busy, I never get to them."

When he got back to his office, the vice president of finance called the staff of the department together and told them he had decided to discontinue this report. They were all shocked. It was their full-time job. He assured them that they would be transferred to other jobs where their work would be more valuable and appreciated, which they were.

Nine months went by. One day, at a company meeting, one of the vice presidents came up to him and asked, "By the way, whatever happened to those reports we used to get every month?"

The vice president of finance said, "We decided to discontinue them."

The executive shrugged and said, "Well, it's no loss. I never had a chance to read them anyway." And that was the end of the matter.

In every company, there are obsolete and unnecessary activities going on that can quite easily be eliminated with no loss or inconvenience to anyone. One of your jobs is to identify them. Find out what they are. And then discontinue them as quickly as possible. Only then will you be able to free up critical resources that you can apply to increasing sales and cash flow for your business.

Simplification in Marketing

The most successful companies are those that have a clear, competitive advantage that they repeat continuously to get their message out to the buying public. It is simple, direct, clear, and benefit-oriented. The more simple your claim for your product or service, your *unique selling proposition*, the easier it is for you to build a marketing and sales campaign around it.

During the business boom in Silicon Valley and the huge infusion of venture capital into dot-com companies, the "elevator pitch" became famous. There were thousands of small companies running around trying to raise money to get started. The venture capitalists with the money were swamped with applications. By one estimate, for every thousand applications a venture capital company received, they considered only one hundred. Of the hundred they considered, they studied only ten. Of the ten proposals they studied, they funded only *one*. The odds of getting financing were very low.

Budding entrepreneurs with new ideas had to condense the essence of their businesses into an "elevator talk" that they would be able to give in a matter of two or three minutes on the elevator from the main office to the ground floor. This elevator talk had to define the potential market, identify the problem that the product or service would solve, spell out the unique selling proposition or special benefit of this particular product or service, and give the market size and financial results possible if this product were successful. All this information had to be conveyed in two to three minutes.

At the height of the dot-com boom, hundreds of dot-com entrepreneurs gathered at special conventions where they received a couple of minutes of time on the stage to pitch their idea to a room full of potential venture capitalists. The ones who could summarize their entire business, including the advantages to the customer of buying and using the product or service, were the ones who had a chance of getting funded.

What is your elevator talk? How could you summarize the benefits and value of what you sell, and why someone should buy it, in two or three minutes? What is your value offering? Why should someone buy your product or service in comparison with every other product or service that is available?

Here's a question for you: "What must your prospective customer *be convinced of* in order to buy your product or service rather than that of any other competitor?"

How can you simplify and focus your advertising, marketing, and sales activities in such a way that you could convince your prospect overwhelmingly that she will get what she wants most from your product or service if she buys it from you?

Simplicity in Selling

In the last fifty years, more than 4,000 books have been written on the subject of selling. Many of them are hundreds of pages long and full of complex strategies, tactics, formulas, methods, and techniques. However, they can all be broken down into three key elements. They are: (1) Prospect; (2) Present; and (3) Follow up and close.

1. Prospecting. This is the beginning of the sales process and the most important part. If you have enough qualified prospects in the front end of your sales pipeline, you will almost inevitably get enough completed sales out of the other end of the pipeline.

A prospect is defined as "someone who can and will buy and pay for your product or service within a reasonable period of time."

A prospect is not someone who likes you or what you sell. It is someone who has the money, the need, and the authority to buy what you sell, combined with an intense desire to enjoy the benefits of your offering as soon as possible.

A good prospect is someone who likes and respects you and your company, wants and needs what you are selling, has the money and the power to make a buying decision, and is ready to move ahead with the buying decision as quickly as possible.

A prospect is not someone who likes you but has no money, no authority, no need, and no urgency. A prospect is not someone who might buy your product or service in a year or two. A prospect is someone who puts food on the table today. Your job is to find as many of them as possible by clearly identifying your ideal prospects and then focusing all of your time, all day long, on speaking to more of these people.

2. Presenting. Presenting is the inner game of selling. Your ability to establish rapport and trust, identify the true problem or needs of the prospect, and then show the prospect that your product or service is, all things considered, the ideal solution for him is the key to sales success.

The good news is that all sales skills are learned. Some of the highest paid and most successful salespeople in the world today could at one time not sell their way across the street. But they settled down and studied selling and the sales profession. They learned the critical skills. They memorized the right questions to ask and the correct responses to customer concerns and objections. They planned their work and worked their plan. As a result, they got better and better, and eventually they sold more and more.

The more of your product you sell, the easier it becomes for you to sell even more of it. You become more knowledgeable and skilled about the sales process. You become more familiar with the most common concerns of the prospects you speak to. Soon you learn how to identify and isolate a good prospect in a few seconds of conversation. You learn how to identify the "hot buttons" of a particular prospect and focus your presentation on satisfying the most important needs he has.

3. Follow Up and Close. In golf they say, "You drive for show but you putt for dough." In sales, you prospect and present for show, but you close for dough. Your ability to overcome the final objections and then get the customer to take action on your offer is the critical part of modern selling.

Take the time to think through and identify your ideal customer, based on the benefits you sell and the needs you satisfy. Use your creativity and imagination to find more and more of these ideal prospects. Learn how to present your product persuasively so that your prospect considers you and your company to be the ideal choice. Finally, learn how to ask for the order and get the customer to make a buying decision.

The more of these three tasks you perform, and the better you get at each one, the simpler and easier selling will be for you, and the more money you will earn.

The Gulf War

During the Gulf War of 1991, the planning was both detailed and simple. The American forces moved what appeared to be massive troop and tank units up to the border with Kuwait. Simultaneously, they moved 17,000 Marines onto ships in the Gulf in preparation for a beach landing in Kuwait City. American intelligence allowed news of these operations to "leak," knowing it would be relayed to Saddam Hussein, who then ordered all his armies forward to defend at the border and the beaches.

In a master stroke of simplicity, General Norman Schwarzkopf then launched his 250,000-man-strong armored divisions across the Iraqi desert in a knockout blow against the town of Basra, thereby cutting off the entire Iraqi army from behind and bringing the war to a swift conclusion.

Simplification and Personal Success

Continually look for ways to reduce the complexity and clutter of your daily life. *If you only had six months left to live, what sort of things would you do, all day long?* This question helps you to identify what is really important to you, what gives you the greatest pleasure and satisfaction when you are not working.

The highest-paid activity in America, and in your life, is *thinking.* The time you take to think about who you are and what you want is more valuable and has a higher payoff to you than any other single activity.

Most people act *impulsively.* The phone rings, someone knocks on the door or comes in, they get an idea or the mail arrives, and they are off! The average person is like a dog that sets off to chase a rabbit across a summer field. As the dog bounds after the rabbit, another rabbit jumps up, and the dog veers after the second rabbit. Then a third rabbit appears, and the dog changes course once more. By the end of the day, the dog has been chasing rabbits back and forth around the field for hours and is completely exhausted. But the dog has caught no rabbits. This is the way many people live their lives.

The opposites of complexity and confusion are focus and concentration. The most important life skill you can develop is the ability to focus single-mindedly on your most important goal or activity and then concentrate completely on achieving that goal. Work without diversion or distraction. Keep coming back to your key task. Discipline yourself to work on your highest payoff activities even when you don't feel like it.

One of the best antidotes to stress is commitment and closure. Commitment means that you make a clear decision that you are going to do something. You then throw your whole heart into doing it quickly and well. Closure means that you discipline yourself to stay at the task until it is 100 percent complete.

You are designed in such a way that you get a tremendous sense of satisfaction and accomplishment whenever you complete an important task. Your brain releases endorphins, which give you a generalized feeling of well-being and happiness. These endorphins cause you to feel more creative and competent. You feel more alert and aware. You feel energized and motivated and eager to tackle new tasks. You trigger these feelings whenever you make yourself complete the most important task you have to do at any given time.

Streamlining and Simplifying Your Life

There are seven ways that you can simplify your life and increase the quality and quantity of your results:

1. Work faster. Get on with it. Develop a *sense of urgency.* Pick up the pace. Whatever you have to do, begin immediately and move quickly from step to step. The very act of moving faster energizes you, increases your creativity, and improves your ability to get even more done.

2. Work longer and harder. Start a little earlier, work a little harder, and stay a little later. Begin your work one hour before anyone else gets there. This allows you to work without interruptions and get a leap on the day. Work at lunchtime when most people are out socializing. This gives you another hour of uninterrupted time to catch up on your tasks and responsibilities. Stay one hour later, after everyone leaves. This enables you to conclude all your work for the day and plan for tomorrow.

By coming in a little earlier, you beat the traffic. By going home a little later, you miss the traffic as well. By working during lunch hour, you stay on top of, and get ahead of, your work and everyone else. In no time at all you will be producing twice as much as the average person, and your paycheck will soon reflect it.

3. Bunch your tasks. When you do several similar tasks together, each subsequent task becomes easier. You get it done faster. Return all your phone calls, one after the other. Answer all of your correspondence, one letter after the other. Do all of your expense reports together. Do all of your business proposals at the same time. Do all of your prospecting at once.

Efficiency experts have discovered that if it takes you *ten* units of time to do the first in a series of similar tasks, it may only take you *two* units of time to do an equal or better job on the fourth or fifth item in that series. This is called the "learning curve," and it is the key to high productivity in every area.

4. Do things you are better at. A small percentage of the things you do account for the majority of the value of all the things you do. There are things that you do in an excellent fashion. When you are working on these tasks, you get more done of higher value, faster and more easily. You contribute greater value in these areas than on any other task.

One of the great secrets of success is for you to do more and more of the things that you are better at and get better and better at these tasks. Simultaneously, do fewer and fewer of the tasks that you are not particularly good at and eventually outsource, delegate, and eliminate them altogether. This will simplify your life and increase your results more than any other strategy.

5. Prepare thoroughly before starting. You've heard the Five P Formula: "Prior Preparation Prevents Poor Performance." It is much easier to focus and concentrate when you have everything you need at your fingertips rather than having to get up and go looking for essential information and materials.

6. Do things together. There are some tasks that you can complete far faster when you do them in cooperation with other people. The entire process of manufacturing is based on the "division of labor," where a task is broken down into smaller chunks allowing each person to specialize in that task. In this way, each person gets onto her own "efficiency curve," becoming more and more efficient at her job. The combined results of several people working together in harmony at specialized tasks can be extraordinary.

The huge Clydesdale horses, famous for pulling the Budweiser beer wagons in the advertisements and commercials, are remarkable examples of the power of teamwork. A single

Clydesdale horse, working alone, can pull a wagon holding 5,000 pounds of freight. Two Clydesdale horses, hitched together and working in tandem, can pull a wagon with 15,000 to 20,000 pounds of freight. But four Clydesdale horses, hitched up and working together can pull as much as 40,000 to 50,000 pounds of freight.

Working together smoothly and efficiently with other people is a "force multiplier" that enables you to accomplish vastly more than if you attempted to do everything by yourself.

7. Simplify your work. Continually look for faster, better, cheaper, and easier ways to accomplish the same task. Reduce complexity. Seek for opportunities to delegate, outsource, and eliminate parts of the work. Simplify your life at every opportunity.

The Principle of Simplicity Revisited

You cannot become more productive by simply increasing the amount of work you do or the number of tasks you complete. There are no courses on time management or personal efficiency that will help you if your goal is simply to get more done with the same amount of time that you have.

The paradoxical fact is this: *You will never get caught up*. You will never get everything done. There is no way that you can complete all of your tasks. You must get this idea out of your mind.

You can only be happier and more productive by simplifying your life. Since you become what you think about, when you think continually about the steps you can take to simplify your activities, you will continually find all kinds of things that you can do to reduce complexity and increase simplicity.

CHAPTER NINE

The Principle of Security

Cover All Your Bases

No operation plan extends with any certainty beyond the first encounter with the main body of the enemy . . . Planning is everything. Plans are nothing.

—FIELD MARSHALL HELMUTH GRAF VON MOLKE,
GERMAN ARMY COMMANDER

Once you have achieved a goal or objective, you must take every precaution necessary to protect and preserve your gains. Top military leaders and executives never allow themselves to become complacent or overconfident. They make provisions to guard against any reversal that might threaten the survival of the army or the enterprise.

The Battle of Chancellorsville

The Battle of Chancellorsville in 1863 was one of the most stunning defeats of a superior force in the Civil War. Robert E. Lee's Army of Northern Virginia was outnumbered two to one by General Joseph Hooker's Union Army of the Potomac. General Hooker was so confident that he made no preparations to defend his right flank. He thought only of moving forward to certain victory.

On the evening of the first day, a farmer came to Robert E. Lee and told him that the Union army's right flank was "hanging in the air." In addition, there was a post road through the tangled brush of the Wilderness area that looped around and emerged at the point where the enemy had prepared no defenses.

Violating one of the core principles of warfare—"Never divide your forces in the face of the enemy"—Lee decided upon a bold and daring move. Holding his position facing the Union army with 17,000 Confederate troops, Lee assigned 30,000 infantry under General Stonewall Jackson to march around to the west and attack the right flank of the Union army on the following day.

After a forced march of several hours, shortly after 5:00 P.M. on May 2, 1863, Jackson's Confederate troops burst out of the tangled undergrowth and attacked in full force. The Union troops, sitting around their campfires preparing dinner, were caught completely unprepared. They reeled frantically backward. By May 4, 1863, the Union Army had beaten a hasty retreat back across the Rappahannock River toward safety. It was a complete disaster for the North. It was caused solely by a single breach of security.

THE PRINCIPLE OF SECURITY:
Never permit the enemy to acquire an unexpected advantage.

Proper security implies that a commander prevents surprise of his own forces, maintains his freedom of action, avoids annoyance by the enemy, and denies information to the enemy. Since risk is inherent in war, application of the principle of security does not imply undue caution and the avoidance of calculated risk. Security can often be enhanced by the seizure and retention of the initiative.

The Principle of Security in Business

The primary job of the executive is to assure the survival of the enterprise. Since all business operations are uncertain and have no guarantee of success, the executive must be continually thinking in terms of survival as well as success.

Sometimes the very best defense is a good offense, as in the case of Robert E. Lee at Chancellorsville. Often the best way to assure your own security is to be aggressively moving ahead, attacking, taking and retaining the initiative, making specific decisions and taking specific actions to assure that you achieve your business objectives and maintain your position in the market.

Putting aside reserves and providing for your financial security always requires both thought and sacrifice. Often, some immediate advantage must be given up to assure longer-term success and survival.

The best leaders are those who take nothing for granted. No matter how successful they are, they remain alert. They guard against the unexpected. They take whatever steps are necessary to guard against a reversal or setbacks. They practice the principle of security.

The Key Question for Security

The principle of security in business requires that you always ask yourself "What is the worst possible thing that could happen in this situation?"

If there are several things that could go wrong, you ask, "Of all the things that could go wrong, what is the *worst* possible single event that could occur to hurt my business or career?"

Excellent leaders practice "crisis anticipation" as a part of daily life. They think continually about the future. They look as far as possible down the road ahead. They continually imagine the various things that could go wrong and think about what they would do to ensure that those things do not happen.

Your ability to achieve and maintain security for yourself and your business is a key leadership quality. It is a vital and active way of thinking and the guarantor against costly setbacks and disappointments. Planning for security can give you the winning edge in a close situation.

Secure Your Competitive Advantage

In business, you identify your most important products and services and the *competitive advantage* that you have in those products and services over your competitors. The best business leaders are adamant about maintaining their positions in the marketplace. They continuously improve the quality of their products and services to ensure that their competitors cannot get ahead of them.

The best companies spend more time and money on research and development of new products and processes than average companies do. They continually upgrade their management information systems and their internal operations. They are determined to stay ahead of their rivals. They leave nothing to chance. They know that their competitors are thinking day and night about taking away their customers and putting them out of business, and they are determined to make sure that that does not happen.

Identify Your Most Vital Customers

The principle of security in business refers, among other things, to sales and cash flow. You must therefore safeguard and protect against the loss of your top customers in every way possible. Once you have made a sale and captured a customer, you must do everything possible to ensure that you keep that customer indefinitely. The cost of acquiring a new customer is ten to fifteen times as much as the cost of servicing an existing customer. Repeat sales from your existing customers have the lowest cost of acquisition and represent the highest profit per sale of any business that you do.

Make it a policy to do everything possible to secure against the loss or disloyalty of your best customers. Many individuals and organizations spend an enormous amount of time and energy to get a customer for the first time, but then they just assume that the customer will stay around. They spend less and less time and energy to keep that customer loyal.

The natural tendency in all relationships is toward *entropy*, a running down of energy and increased disorder. Entropy in sales and marketing refers to the tendency to take your customers for granted once you have acquired them. This can be fatal. Many companies have actually gone out of business as the result of losing a major customer, or customer group, that they stopped paying attention to.

You should spend a full third of your advertising and promotional expenses on your most recent customers. These are the ones who are the most likely to buy again and to tell their friends.

Two Types of Customers

There are always two groups of customers in your market. There are, first of all, those customers who know you and like you. They have bought from you in the past and are happy with the way you have taken care of them. These are the customers who buy from you again and are the best sources of references and referrals. These are the lowest-cost, lowest-maintenance, highest-profit customers you have. They are the mainstays of your business.

The second category of customers is those people who have never heard of you and have no idea or knowledge of what you do or why they should buy from you. The mistake that many companies make is that they focus most of their advertising and sales efforts on those customers who couldn't care less about them rather than aiming their efforts at those customers who already know and like them.

Secure Your Main Customers

When you ask yourself "What is the worst possible thing that could happen in my business?," think in terms of your customers. What would happen if you were to lose one or more of your main customers? What kind of impact would it have on your sales, your income, and your cash flow? If the loss of one of your major customers represents a serious danger to you, what steps could you take immediately to assure that you do not lose that customer in the first place? Be aware of any potential weaknesses in your marketing strategy. Often you lose a customer because your basic assumptions are wrong.

The Battle of Quebec

In 1759, France and the French armies were in control of Quebec, their position of superiority protected by the fortress of Quebec on a promontory overlooking the St. Lawrence River.

The fort was virtually unassailable by land. As long as the French held the position with its huge cannons, the British could not move up the river to achieve their desired domination of Canada.

The only approach to the fort that was undefended was the high cliff overlooking the river. It was so steep that it was considered to be unclimbable. This assumption turned out to be their downfall.

An Indian scout with the British army came to the commanding general, James Wolfe, and told him of a little-known path that led up the cliff to the plain before the fort. That night, the entire British army, one man at a time, climbed the narrow path and emerged on the plain in front of the fort. When the sun arose the next morning, the British army was arrayed in full battle formation on the Plains of Abraham and ready to give battle.

The French General, Montcalm, who had placed no sentries on the cliff, assumed that this was merely a small skirmishing party. He led his soldiers out of the fort to give battle and drive them off. On that day, September 13, 1759, there were some preliminary skirmishes, and then suddenly both forces were fully engaged. A fierce ten-minute battle took place during which Generals Wolfe and Montcalm were both killed, and the French army was defeated.

This battle and the British victory, made possible by a single breach in the security of the French position, brought to an end the dreams of a French empire in the New World and canceled out 150 years of time and investment by France in North America.

The Stakes Are High

Business is similar to warfare in that the stakes can be very high. Victory and defeat are always possible. Your competition is determined to win your customers and gain the revenues and profits that go along with them. Your competition never sleeps. Your counterparts at competing organizations are continually thinking about how they can outmaneuver you and get at your customers. They plan and strategize to take them away and to keep them indefinitely. They want to seize and hold your markets. You must think the same way—and better.

In business, the only real security you can ever have is your ability to serve your customers better than your competitors do. Your security comes from your ability to determine *exactly* what it is that your customers want and are willing to pay for and then to give it to them faster and better than your competitors possibly could.

Your Most Valuable Asset

The most valuable asset of any company is its reputation in the marketplace, how it is *known* to its customers. The most valuable asset of your company is contained in the way your customers think and talk about your company when you are not there. Your company's reputation, what people say about your company to other customers and prospects, is the key determinant of how secure your company's position is in today's marketplace.

The most successful companies invest a good deal of time and effort in their advertising, promotion, and public relations to assure that their customers, and potential customers think highly of them whenever they think about the products and services that they sell.

The Power of Reputation

Not long ago, a public opinion survey was conducted in Phoenix, Arizona. Shoppers were asked their opinions of various department stores. "Which department store do you feel offers the best combination of quality and service to its customers?"

It was not surprising that Nordstrom's stores won 50 percent of the votes in the customer survey. Fully 50 percent of shoppers rated Nordstrom above all other department stores in the Phoenix area for its quality and service. Nordstrom's reputation for customer service is the best of any department store in the country.

What was surprising however was that in Phoenix, Arizona, there was no Nordstrom store. The only experience that Phoenix shoppers had with Nordstrom's was when they visited a Nordstrom store in California and then came home and told their friends about their experience.

The reputation of Nordstrom's for quality products and service was so great that customers who did not even shop at Nordstrom's rated it above the stores that they did patronize on a regular basis. This is the kind of reputation that translates into extraordinary success in the marketplace. You should be continually thinking about the things that you can do in the operation of your own business to create such a positive reputation that your customers are naturally drawn to preferring your offerings over those of your competitors.

The Battle of Waterloo

The Battle of Waterloo, fought on June 18, 1815, was perhaps the largest and most decisive battle that had been fought on the European continent at that time. Because of Napoleon's more than twenty years of brilliant military successes, the Duke of Wellington was the underdog going into the battle. The fate and future of the French Empire, the Prussian Empire, the Austrian Empire, and the British position in Europe all hung in the balance.

But even though the stakes were extremely high, and the odds were against him, Wellington took badly needed troops out of his main army and posted them as a reserve on the road to Brussels in the event that he was defeated on the battlefield. Wellington knew that, without a reserve, if the French overwhelmed his army, it could be destroyed as a fighting force and be incapable of regrouping and fighting again later. In Wellington's mind, an orderly defeat was preferable to a complete disaster.

Meanwhile, the French committed their entire army at the Battle of Waterloo. They threw in every infantry and cavalry regiment and division. When the battle turned against them at the end of the day with the arrival of the Prussian troops under Blücher to support Wellington, the French had no reserves left. As a result, the French army was routed and destroyed as a fighting force in Europe. Napoleon was defeated. France was not able to recover as a military power for another hundred years. It had failed to secure against a possible reversal of fortune.

Expect the Best, Plan for the Worst

Bernard Baruch, the famous financier, once said, "When business is good for any period of time, eventually people come to believe that business will always be good. When business is poor for any period of time, people eventually come to believe that business will always be poor. Neither is correct. Business fluctuates."

Run your business like a military force surrounded by the enemy. Like Wellington, you should plan for eventual victory but provide necessary reserves in case of unexpected reversals. Protect your flanks. Take whatever steps are necessary to assure the survival of your enterprise, no matter what happens. Even when business is excellent, remain alert and prepared for possible reversals or downturns. Business always fluctuates.

Begin the process of securing your future by developing accurate and conservative cash projections for the next six to twelve months. How much do you have? How much will you need? Develop high-, medium-, and low-range estimates of sales, revenues, and profitability. Always ask, "What is the worst possible thing that could happen *financially* in the coming year?" Whatever it might be, provide reserves to guard against any unexpected decline in sales and revenue.

Identify your key sources of sales, and your most important customer groups. What are your best-selling products and services? Who are the most important individuals or organizations that buy from you? What can you do today to secure and protect these sources of business? Never forget that the purpose of a company is *to create and keep a customer.* You must pay as much attention to keeping customers as you do to acquiring them in the first place.

Think about your key sources of money and your most important banking relationships. What would happen if your lines of credit were cut off for any reason? What could you do to guard against any problems with your bank?

When we were kids, there was a rule in our family: "Beat the news home." This meant that if you got into trouble in the neighborhood or at school, you had to make sure that you were the first person to tell your parents. Never let them find out from someone else first.

In your business and personal life, this is an important rule for dealing with your bank or any institution that supplies you with money. If there is a problem of any kind, "Beat the news home." Be the first one to tell them that there is a shortfall. The most important rule in dealing with banks is: "No surprises!" Surprises with regard to money are very seldom *positive* surprises.

How can you strengthen your banking and financial relationships? How can you improve them? What alternatives do you have if the worst should occur? Hope is not a strategy. Remember that, "An ounce of prevention is better than a pound of cure."

Your business should be fully *insured* against every emergency for which you cannot sit down and write a check. Use a good insurance broker to help identify every business activity in which you could be vulnerable to loss, litigation, or lawsuit of any kind. With the tort system as out of control as it is today, you must take every precaution. One of the smartest things you can do is to purchase *liability* insurance to protect yourself against someone claiming damage or injury from some activity of your business or your staff. Fortunately, liability insurance of this kind is relatively inexpensive.

Identify Your Key People

The value of your business comes from the people who work there. Identify the key people who add the most to your company's value and then ask yourself, "What would I do if I were to lose one or more of these people?"

Practice *scenario planning* regularly. Look into the future and identify the most harmful events that could possibly occur regarding not only your key people but every aspect of your business.

Foresight refers to your ability to think ahead well into the future and accurately anticipate what might happen to help you or hurt you in the months and years ahead. Even if an occurrence has only a small probability of happening, if the negative effects of that event could be severe enough, you should think about how you can guard against it. You should always be mentally prepared for any setback or reversal. This is the hallmark of the excellent leader.

"Patience and foresight are the two most important qualities in business."

—HENRY FORD

The Evaluation of Risk

Because all of business life is fraught with *uncertainty*, you cannot avoid taking risks almost every single day. However, you should evaluate each risk and place it into one of the following categories:

First, there are the risks that *you must take* to stay in business. These involve hiring and assigning people to specific tasks, advertising and promotion, investment in new product development, committing expenditures to develop new sources of business, and so on. These are essential risks that go with the territory of running a modern business. They are unavoidable.

Second, there are the risks that *you can afford to take*. These are actions and decisions for which there is no guaranteed outcome but for which you can absorb their cost as a part of doing business if they are not successful. Bringing a new product or service to the market or running an advertisement in an untested medium is a risk that you can afford to take. If the actions fail, they will not threaten the survival of your enterprise.

The third type of risk is the risk that *you cannot afford to take*. The cost is too high. The consequences of failure may sink your business. Even though such risks offer extraordinary upside potential, their downside potential may be so severe that it is better to pass on them when they arise. Survival of the enterprise must be your overriding consideration.

A risk that you cannot afford to take would be an investment of so much money that its failure would cause your company to go bankrupt. In almost every risky situation, the potential benefits can be extremely attractive. But paying close attention to the potential downfalls will give you the security that you need to remain in operation. Be willing to say "No!"

Finally, there are the risks that *you cannot afford **not** to take*. There are many activities in the operation of your business that entail high degrees of uncertainty, but you must engage in them anyway. A risk that you cannot afford not to take may be entering into a strategic alliance with another company to counter a competitor who threatens the sales of your main products or services. There is no guarantee that this decision will be successful but often you cannot afford not to do it if you want to stay in business.

Security in business requires that you continually ask, "What could possibly go wrong?" Whatever your answer to that question, make provisions to secure against the worst possible outcome. This enables you to sleep well at night and to concentrate your energies on business success during the day.

The Principle of Security in Personal Success

Your goals in personal life are to be successful, happy, healthy, and prosperous. Your goals are to fulfill your full potential and become everything that you are capable of becoming. Your aim is not just to live, but to live a great life. One of the most important principles for assuring that you accomplish all of these is the practice of the principle of security in everything you do.

The need for security is one of the deepest and most profound needs we have. The psychologist Abraham Maslow concluded that our needs for *security*—financial, emotional, physical—are so vital that, when our security is threatened for any reason, we think of nothing else. Our security needs preoccupy us completely.

You could be going along quite happily in your life, quite content and having few problems. Then, one day, you go into work in the morning and someone tells you that the company will be laying off 50 percent of the staff, and no one knows which 50 percent it will be.

From being happy and confident, you could immediately become scared and nervous. Before, your life was flowing along like "Old Man River," but now your financial security is threatened. Suddenly, from not thinking about it at all, you will begin to think and talk about nothing else. Until the decision is made about who will be laid off, you will be totally preoccupied with this threat to your security.

Or you could be enjoying your life and giving very little thought to your health. You then go in for a medical check-up.

Your doctor comes back and tells you that there is something in the test that looks suspicious and that an exploratory surgery will be necessary to find out if there is anything to worry about.

Suddenly, with your physical health threatened, you will become totally preoccupied with what the medical tests might indicate. This threat to your health or your life can become so overwhelming that you will think and talk about nothing else until you know the results, one way or another.

The Importance of Options

You are only as free as your options. You are only as free as your well-developed alternatives to whatever you are doing today. If you have only one choice, or one course of action you can take, you will start to feel trapped. You will feel locked in and out of control of your life or your situation. You will begin to experience what Dr. Martin Seligman of the University of Pennsylvania calls "learned helplessness." You will feel unable to change or improve your condition. This feeling causes inordinate stress and anxiety.

Throughout your life, one of your most important strategies is the systematic development of *options*. You must continually expand the range of possibilities open to you. You must never allow yourself to be trapped in a situation from which you have made no provision for escape.

For example, the better you are at what you do, the more job options you have. The healthier you are, the more different options you have for physical activities. The more people you know, and who know you, the greater will be your options in your personal and social life. When you accumulate money in the bank, you expand your range of options as well.

Continually ask yourself, "If I lost my job and all my money today, what would I do?" Your answer to this question will tell you how many well-developed options you have. Your ability to develop additional options throughout your life is essential for a feeling of freedom, happiness, self-reliance, and personal power.

Your Most Valuable Personal Asset

What is your most valuable asset in business and in life? What is your most valuable asset as an individual? Just as a company's most valuable asset is its *reputation*, this is your most valuable asset as well. The way people think and talk about you when you are not there is the most important single determinant of how successful you will be in whatever you do. The most successful business people and salespeople are thought of highly and talked about in complimentary terms by other people when they are not present.

What do people think and say about you in your absence? What would you like them to say? Your ability to influence and shape people's perceptions of you in a positive way is a key to the security of your position and your income in today's competitive world.

The Only Security You Can Ever Have

Abraham Lincoln once said, "The only security you can ever have is the ability to do your job uncommonly well." We are rapidly moving out of the "Age of the Job" and into the "Age of the Independent Contractor." To succeed in your work today, you must continually see yourself as *self-employed*, as the president of your own personal services corporation. When you work, imagine that you are selling your services on a daily basis, as a consultant would do, to your employer. Imagine that your employer is evaluating your work on a daily basis to determine whether or not to keep you on for an additional day or week. Even better, imagine that you are being paid on an hourly basis, and you have to make every hour count.

When you begin treating every hour as an hour that has to count in terms of *unique added value* to your employer, you will find yourself using your time much better and producing much more than the people around you. You will be creating the very best form of job and income security possible.

The rule for success at work has always been: "Get good, get better, be the best!" Your central focus should be to make yourself first valuable and then indispensable. You should do your work in such a way that your company would really suffer if you weren't there.

In a competitive economy, you most often achieve your goals by daring to go forward, by seizing the initiative, by going on the offensive. You achieve your economic and financial security by continuously upgrading your knowledge and skills so that you get ahead, and stay ahead, of your competitors, both inside and outside your company.

The Winning-Edge Theory

The winning-edge theory of success says that small differences in ability can translate into large differences in results. Identify the skills that you can develop in which small increases in your ability can translate into enormous differences in the results you get and the contribution you make. Identify your areas of weakness in your job, and make a plan to strengthen yourself in those areas.

Achieving Financial Security

Perhaps the most important part of security in your personal life is your ability to achieve and maintain your own financial security. Your goal is to reach the point where you never have to worry about money again. You want to be able to order in a restaurant without looking at the right-hand column to see how hungry you are. You want to get far enough ahead financially so that no matter what happens in your life, you are financially secure and you can relax.

The only way to achieve financial security is for you to become extremely good at what you do and then become well-paid for doing it. Small differences in performance can translate into enormous differences in results and rewards. Your responsibility is to read the books, take the courses, and listen to the audio programs. Your goal is to continually improve in your work so that you eventually join the top 10 percent of money earners in your field, whatever your job may be.

Financial Success at Your Fingertips

It has never been more possible for you to achieve financial independence than it is today. There are more opportunities for you to increase your income and to accumulate wealth today than have ever existed before. And there are no limits except the limits in your own mind.

To attain long-term financial security, there is a simple five-word formula, *Spend Less Than You Earn.* If you do this consistently and in sufficient quantity throughout your life, you will achieve financial independence or even more. If you do not spend less than you earn, you will always have money worries and you will never be secure or happy.

Your goal should be to build a financial fortress around your life. To build this fortress, you must save your money, every paycheck, every month, every year, throughout your working lifetime. You must set financial goals, make plans and work on your plans, day in and day out, month in and month out, year in and year out, until you have finally reached the point where you never have to worry about money again.

There are more than five million millionaires in America today, most of them self-made. Experts predict that the number of millionaires in America will double again in the next ten years. Today, somewhere in America, someone becomes a new millionaire every four-and-a-half minutes, twenty-four hours a day, 365 days a year, and the rate is increasing.

For every millionaire, there are many others who are achieving net worths in the hundreds of thousands of dollars. There are many people who have achieved net worths of several million dollars, several hundred million dollars, a billion dollars, and even many billions of dollars, most of them self-made, starting from little or nothing earlier in life.

The Formula for Financial Security

The rule for financial independence has always been the same. It comes from George S. Clason's "Richest Man in Babylon." Of every dollar you earn, 10 percent is yours to keep.

Your goal should be to save at least 10 percent of your income, and preferably 15 percent or 20 percent of your income, over the course of your working lifetime.

Albert Einstein once said that the greatest power in the human universe is *the power of compound interest*. It is also the key to financial independence. If you were to save just $100 per month from the age of twenty to the age of sixty-five, and if that $100 per month were to grow at a compound rate of 10 percent per annum, which is reasonably conservative, you would be worth well over one million dollars when you retire.

Compound interest grows very slowly in the beginning but then begins to increase with the force of an avalanche moving down a mountain. A dollar invested at 3 percent interest at the time of Christ would be worth half the money in the world today.

If you took a penny and you doubled that penny every day for thirty days, it would be worth millions of dollars. But if you took a penny and doubled it every day and then, after ten days, you took the money and spent it, it would only be worth a few dollars. Unfortunately, this is what most people do with their savings.

All serious money is patient money. All serious money is based on *long-term perspective*. Men and women who achieve financial independence are those who think long-term and who are willing to make sacrifices in the short term in order to make their financial dreams come true.

All of life is a series of *trade-offs*. The most successful people trade short-term pain for long-term gain. They are willing to sacrifice in the short term in order to enjoy even greater benefits in the long term. They practice delayed gratification, the key to economic success in life. Successful people are willing to pay the price of success in advance and to put off the enjoyment of immediate rewards and benefits to ensure that even greater rewards and benefits will be available later.

The Habits of Millionaires

In Thomas J. Stanley and William D. Danko's best-selling book, *The Millionaire Next Door*, they reveal their finding that the key difference between men and women who achieve financial independence and those who do not is that the financially successful prefer financial independence to status and current consumption. Financial independence comes about as a result of being careful with every dollar. You become wealthy as the result of being frugal with your money as you move toward your goal of financial independence.

Self-made millionaires prefer the pleasure of having money in the bank to the pleasure of having a good time as they go along. They never buy when they can lease. They never lease when they can rent. They never rent when they can borrow. And they never buy it new when they can get it used.

The Measure of Financial Security

Perhaps the key measure of how well you are doing financially comes out of interviews with self-made millionaires. When asked how they measure financial success, self-made millionaires invariably refer to their "run rate."

Your *run rate* is defined as the number of months and years that you could support your current standard of living without ever working again. Financially independent people have a run rate that extends beyond their expected lifetimes. In other words, they could stop working today and they could enjoy their current standard of living for the rest of their lives with the amount they have accumulated.

Here is a good question for you: What is your *personal* run rate? In other words, how long could you live comfortably without working, subsisting entirely on your existing savings and investments?

Fully 70 percent of adults today have no run rate at all. The great majority of people are only two months away from homelessness. Many people with high incomes have no savings at all. Even worse, they have mortgages, rents, expenses, and high levels of debt that they have to service every month.

A friend of mine is the head of a large accounting firm. His company does the bookkeeping and tax preparation for several very wealthy people. He told me that he had noticed a quality that they all had in common. They all seemed to have *low levels of debt*. They had their money carefully diversified and invested in a variety of different areas. They did not spend extravagantly on yachts, vacation homes, private planes, luxury goods, or other trappings of wealth. Instead, they seemed to stay close to the ground. They lived in nice neighborhoods in reasonably priced homes.

Most self-made millionaires in America appear to be just average people on the outside. They do not display their wealth to others. Even their children do not know how much money they are worth. They never talk about it or show it off. They are not concerned with status at all. They are more concerned with financial security. They are interested in securing their position.

The Patton Principle

General George S. Patton, Jr. was adamant about not paying for the same ground twice. He insisted that once his troops had taken a particular objective, they secure the objective so strongly that it could not be retaken by German counterattack. Patton was determined that, whatever it cost in men and matériel to obtain an objective, his army would not have to pay that cost again because of a failure to take the necessary precautions to secure their position.

Building Your Financial Fortress

Many people have savings accounts, but people who become wealthy have different attitudes toward their savings accounts than people who do not. People who become wealthy save their money but they never, *never* touch it or spend it on current expenditures. People who don't become wealthy may save their money as well, at least temporarily, but they are always looking for opportunities to buy something with the money they have put away. If you use up the money in your savings account, you are losing the ground you have gained. Think instead like Patton and try to secure that money instead of wasting it.

The rule is that, once you have begun accumulating money to build your financial fortress and increase your run rate, you never touch the money for any reason. If you want to save money for a car or a motor home or a trip, you open up a separate account and you put money into that account for that reason.

Your financial fortress account, however, is where you put your money away, and you never think of spending it except on long-term investments that will become the bricks in the financial fortress that you are constructing around yourself.

The Rules of Money and Investment

The rules and money and investment have never changed. First of all, money goes and stays where it is *appreciated*. Money seems to have a personality, and it is attracted to people who love it and care about it.

Here is a simple test for how much you appreciate your money. Look at the money you have in your pocket, your wallet, or your purse. Is it neatly organized or is it all mixed up?

Are your various bills organized by denomination, with each of the heads facing in the same direction, or are your bills like a deck of shuffled cards with no order or sequence? Look at your checkbook. Is it carefully organized and properly balanced, or is it hopelessly confused? These are indications of how much you appreciate your money. They will also tell you how financially successful you are today.

Second, financially successful people are very careful with their money. They know exactly how much they have, and they plan their expenditures carefully. They have their money properly organized. They spend about ten to twenty hours each month thinking about and planning their financial life. They take nothing for granted. They are not casual about something that is so important to their security as their financial situation.

On the other hand, people with financial problems are usually uncertain about how much money they have, how much things really cost, how much they are paying, and how much they are worth. As a result of this confusion in their financial lives, they have continuous feelings of insecurity about their money and their future, which are probably well-deserved.

Make a Decision

Make a decision today to get all of your financial affairs in order. Imagine that you were going to pass away tomorrow morning and that someone was going to have to come in and sort out your finances quickly and efficiently for your family and friends. Organize your finances in such a way that they are summarized and correct, and every detail is properly organized, so that a third party could understand your financial situation immediately. The very act of sitting down and analyzing your financial situation from beginning to end will enable you to impose order on your financial life and start you on your upward journey to financial independence.

How to Become Wealthy

To become wealthy, you should save and invest 10 percent or more of your income, every single paycheck. For most people, it is usually not possible for them to begin saving 10 percent of their income at the beginning. Most people's financial lives are out of control. They have more month at the end of the money than they have money at the end of the month. They are in a constant state of juggling bills and credit card payments. This may be your situation at the moment as well.

If you cannot save 10 percent of your income, make a decision today to save one percent of your income each month. If you earn $2,000 a month, open up a special bank account and begin depositing $20 a month (1 percent) into it immediately. The sooner you get started, the sooner you will become financially independent. You discipline yourself to live on the other 99 percent of your income. This is fairly easy.

Once you feel comfortable saving one percent of your income, increase it to two percent and live on the other 98 percent. Then increase your savings rate to 3 percent, then 4 percent, and so on. Within a year, you will be saving 10 percent or 15 percent, of your income off the top of every paycheck. In three to five years, you will have a substantial sum of money put away.

The Law of Attraction applies to money. *Money attracts more money.* The more you save and accumulate, the more money you will attract to you to save and accumulate. The better you become at managing your finances, the more finances you will have to manage. The more responsible you become with regard to your money, the more money you will have to be responsible for. This is a universal rule that never varies.

Invest Your Money Carefully

Spend as much time studying an investment of your money as you spent earning the money. *Investigate before you invest.* Study every detail of the proposal. Never invest in anything that you do not thoroughly understand and agree with.

Self-made millionaires do not gamble, speculate, or take chances. They do not lose money. Self-made millionaires would rather keep the money in the bank at interest than take a chance at losing it. They have worked too hard to accumulate it in the first place.

To achieve financial security, invest with *experts* with proven success records investing their own money. Don't invest in other people's ideas or other people's businesses where there is no track record of success. Ninety-nine percent of all entrepreneurial ventures eventually fail, taking all the money down with them.

The Principle of Security Revisited

One of the keys to happiness, health, and long life is for you to achieve your own financial security. This happens when you become very good at what you do and then become very well paid for doing it. Out of your increasing income, you then save 10 percent, 15 percent, and 20 percent out of every single paycheck. You put this money away and you never touch it except to invest it carefully with experts who have proven track records.

You delay the purchase of status symbols like expensive cars, jewelry, clothes, motor homes, and boats in the short term, so that you can achieve real wealth in the long term. You concentrate on building your savings and investment account so that you ultimately achieve a run rate of twenty years or more.

Once you have built your financial fortress—and this requires tremendous discipline and willpower on your part—you will become one of the happiest, healthiest, and most positive people in your world. You will have the admiration, respect, and esteem of all the people around you.

You will have achieved one of the most important victories possible in modern life. You will have achieved your own financial security and you will be unstoppable.

CHAPTER TEN

The Principle of Economy
Conserve Your Resources

Always remember that it is much better to waste ammunition than lives.

—GENERAL GEORGE S. PATTON

E ffective leaders conserve their resources. They carefully estimate in advance what something is likely to cost and what it is likely to gain. They pay full measure for their successes, but not more. They weigh and compare each expenditure against the possible rewards and are willing to pass on an opportunity if they cannot justify the cost of taking advantage of it.

The Battle of Asculum

At Asculum in 279 B.C., the Greek King Pyrrhus defeated a Roman army in a pitched battle at a cost of more than one third of his army. When he was congratulated for his victory, he said, "Alas, one more such victory and we are lost."

He had won a victory, but at such a high cost that it was not worth what he had lost to achieve it. His forces were substantially weakened. He could not rebuild his army quickly enough.

The Romans immediately sent another army against him, and in the ensuing battle, his forces were destroyed, his empire was lost, and he was killed. His success at such a high cost had led to his ultimate defeat. His first victory became forever known as a "Pyrrhic victory." He had won initially but at such a cost that he was eventually destroyed. Many companies spend so much in achieving market position that they no longer have the financial resources to continue.

> **The Principle of Economy of Force: Allocate minimum essential combat power to secondary efforts.**

This principle is a corollary to the principle of the mass, for it is a method of achieving mass. And like the principle of the mass, the principle of economy of force requires the commander to choose the time and place for secondary efforts and to determine the amount of physical resources that comprise minimum essential combat power at that time and place. Inherent in both the principle of the mass and the principle of economy of force is the idea that all available resources must be employed in the most efficient and effective manner.

This principle is essential to success in business and in warfare. Only by conserving resources can the commander assemble sufficient mass to achieve victory against the primary objectives.

The Principle of Economy in Business

Your ability to achieve your primary and secondary objectives at the lowest possible cost is essential to your success in business. The first principle of economics is that critical resources are scarce. There are never enough of them. You never have enough time, enough money, enough talent, or enough of anything of value. You must always conserve and economize and never pay more than is necessary to achieve a particular business result.

All of economics is aimed at increasing the quantity of outputs relative to inputs. In other words, you want to get more out relative to the amount you put in. The principle of economy applies to your work in that the most successful executives are those who are able to achieve the highest quantity of results at the lowest actual cost in time and money. This must be an essential part of your thinking throughout your business career; otherwise, you will waste critical resources that might be necessary in future battles.

The Battle of Cold Harbor

On June 3, 1864, Lieutenant General Ulysses S. Grant, commander of the Union army, launched a concentrated attack to break the Confederate lines at Cold Harbor, Virginia. This frontal attack across open land against entrenched positions was repulsed with 12,000 Union soldiers killed or wounded. In exchange for these horrendous casualties, the Union achieved nothing. No ground was gained. The Confederate army remained solidly in position. All the men and matériel involved were wasted.

The Principles of Economics

Sometimes I offer to teach my audiences the basic principles of economics in less than five minutes. After twenty-five years and many thousands of hours studying the subject, I have concluded that all economic decisions revolve around four or five basic ideas, with a series of additional concepts and principles added in for explanation.

Here is my "Economics in Five Minutes" lesson; it consists of a series of questions and answers.

My first question is this: "If I could offer you either $10,000 dollars per year or $100,000 per year to do the same job, which salary would you choose?"

The usual answer is that almost everyone would choose to earn $100,000 per year rather than $10,000 for the same job. This is normal, natural, and logical. All people prefer *more to less*, all things being equal. Sometimes politicians and others claim that people are "greedy." But people are not greedy. They just prefer more to less. This is a basic characteristic of human nature and has been true throughout the history of humankind.

My second question is this: "If you could receive this $100,000 on January 1 or December 31 of the same year, when would you like to have it?"

Everyone usually answers that they would prefer to receive the money on January 1 rather than December 31. This is because everyone prefers *sooner to later*. Given a choice, all things being equal, you will always prefer to have a benefit earlier rather than having to wait for it. You are naturally impatient, just like everyone else.

Sometimes people are criticized for being impatient and greedy with regard to getting the things they want. But this is not true. People simply prefer more to less and sooner to later.

The third question I ask is this: "If you could earn this $100,000 per year doing an easy job or a difficult job, which type of job would you prefer?"

As you might expect, everyone chooses the easy job over the harder job. This is another normal characteristic of human nature and explains a basic principle of economics. Everyone prefers easier rather than harder when given a choice. Sometimes people are accused of being "lazy." But people are not lazy. They just prefer an easier way to a harder way in achieving the same result, all things being equal.

The final question I ask is: "If you could be absolutely guaranteed of this amount of money or if your receiving this money was highly uncertain, which would you choose?"

In this case, virtually everyone chooses a *higher* degree of certainty rather than a *lower* degree of certainty. As we mentioned in the previous chapter, security is a basic human need, and the desire for security is a characteristic of human nature.

These four answers tell you most of what you need to know about human activity in general and about economics in particular. Virtually everyone you know, including your customers, prefers more to less, sooner rather than later, easier rather than more difficult, and with greater certainty rather than uncertainty.

Every decision that anyone makes with regard to any expenditure of time, money, or emotion takes these four factors into consideration.

If you are in sales, every customer that you deal with is seeking to get more of what they want, sooner, easier, and with greater certainty. In a competitive market, your ability to convince your customer that your product or service offers the very best likelihood of achieving these four factors plus getting the specific benefits of what you sell is the key to market success.

Two Critical Factors in Decision-Making

There are two factors concerning time that determine the purchase of any product or service in a competitive marketplace. The first is called "time to market." If you can get your product or service to the market faster than your competitor, or if you can offer a benefit that people want and are willing to pay for more quickly than someone else, you can leapfrog your competition and get the sale. Everybody prefers sooner to later, and the companies and individuals who do things quickly and produce products and services faster are always more respected and better rewarded than those who are slower.

The second factor that determines virtually all business purchases, and many other purchases as well, is called "time to payback."

Time to payback refers to the amount of time that a customer anticipates waiting before she gets a sufficient return on her investment in the product or service to justify having bought it in the first place.

In business, this is often called the "internal rate of return" (IRR).

The internal rate of return is the percentage of return that a customer receives as the result of using the product or service that you are selling.

For example, when Xerox released the first two-sided copying machines, their marketing specialists developed a sales presentation that enabled their salespeople to sell the machines in large quantities. They sat down with a prospective customer, usually a decision-maker in the printing and mailing department of a large company, and conducted an economic analysis of their photocopying and mailing costs. They demonstrated to the prospective customer that, by copying on both sides of the sheet of paper, they could cut their mailing costs in half. The savings on mailing costs for a large company turned out to be greater than the entire cost of the photocopier. In fact, as soon as the company began using the two-sided copier, they began to make a profit or a return on investment in excess of the total cost of the copier, paper, toner, and maintenance. This made the decision easy.

The Question You Must Answer

Every customer wants to know, "What's in it for me?" in terms of economic advantage and bottom-line benefit.

Every purchaser wants to know how *fast* he gets the return that you promise. Every purchaser wants to know how *certain* it is that he will receive that return. Your job as a professional salesperson is to demonstrate to a prospective purchaser that he will get a return that is greater, faster, easier, and more certain from *your* product or service than he would receive from someone else's product or service or from doing nothing at all.

In a sense, your job is to demonstrate that you sell "free" products to qualified business customers. Your job is to show that the purchaser more than pays for your product or service with the profit or savings that she realizes from using it. If a company pays 10 percent to borrow money from the bank and you can demonstrate that your product or service will pay for itself in five years, the equivalent of a 20 percent internal rate of return, then what you are selling is actually a profit maker for the customer. Your product turns out to be "free" over time. In this case, the only question that the customer will have is, "How certain can I be that your promises and projections will be achieved?" If you can't ensure that your projections will be achieved, they risk losing resources for nothing. The key is to convince the customers that they can achieve their main objective—to make a profit—by using your product. You need to convince them that they can conserve their resources by using your product.

Operation Desert Storm

Operation Desert Storm in 1991 was a classic example of the application of the principle of the economy of force. By preceding the ground attack with intensive laser-guided aerial bombardment, the allies were able to knock out the complete command and control structure of the Iraqi army. They were able to destroy hundreds of tanks and artillery pieces. They were able to virtually eliminate the Iraqi army's ability to defend or counterattack effectively.

When the main allied ground attack, "Desert Sabre," was launched, the battle was over in 104 hours, with a total loss of fewer than 200 men on the allied side. The Iraqi army lost as many as 50,000 dead. In terms of *economy*, it was one of the best-fought and lowest-cost victories ever attained in the history of warfare.

The Principle of Economy and Money

The principle of economy applied to your business means that you must conserve cash at all times. Cash is like blood to the brain. It is essential for survival. A company with high sales but no cash can go out of business. A company with low sales but ample cash reserves can survive even the toughest economic times.

Take every opportunity to build up and put cash reserves aside. Never allow yourself to run out of money. The difference between having money in the bank and scrambling for enough cash to cover payroll is the difference between night and day.

"Never yield ground. It is cheaper to hold what you have than to retake what you have lost."

—GENERAL GEORGE S. PATTON

One way to build reserves is to reduce costs of operation. The best companies, even when business is going well, are always looking for ways to reduce expenses. Resolve to run a tight ship. Question every expense. Delay, defer, and procrastinate on major expenses when you possibly can.

Before you buy anything, research it thoroughly to make sure that you actually need it and that the price you are getting is the very best available. Do careful financial analysis before you make any commitment. When in doubt, put off the decision. Never allow yourself to be rushed into spending money that weakens your cash situation.

When you are growing your business, you should only incur expenses on things that can have a direct influence on increasing sales and revenues. Many young companies make the mistake of spending money on furniture, fixtures, and offices before they begin making profits. All of these expenditures require cash. Again and again, when the company gets into a cash crunch, it often goes under because all the cash has already been spent and new cash is unavailable.

The Battle of Verdun

During World War I, the German and French forces had been locked in a stalemate of trench warfare for almost two years—each side losing hundreds of thousands of men with no gains in territory. At the Battle of Verdun, which lasted from February until December, 1916, the German commander von Falkenhayn planned a massive offensive to overwhelm once and for all the French forces arrayed against him.

After a massive nine-hour artillery barrage, fired by 1,400 guns, he launched three corps of the German Fifth Army, several hundred thousand men, in an attack along an eight-mile front. The French forces reeled backward, and the Germans surged forward, overwhelming the French front lines.

Then the French army under the command of General Pétain counterattacked, stopping the German advances. A battle of attrition followed. For the next nine months, each attack was followed by a counterattack, back and forth, by both sides. When the battle finally ended in December 1916, both armies were back to where they had started in the spring. France had suffered more than 500,000 casualties, and Germany had lost more than 434,000 men. Almost a million young men had been destroyed with no gain or advantage by either side. This is one of the worst violations of the principle of economy in military history.

The Turnaround Strategy

Treat your company like a turnaround at all times. Imagine that your company is on the verge of bankruptcy. If you were out of money, what actions would you take immediately in order to survive? What expenses would you slash? Where would you cut back or reduce outlays?

The best managers in the best-managed companies practice tight financial discipline at all times. No matter how much they earn in profits, they watch every penny of expenditure. This attitude of the top managers spreads throughout the company and motivates everyone else to be careful about expenditures as well.

Determine Your Breakeven Point

Imagine that your sales stopped suddenly for a month or more. How much does it cost you to keep your doors open without sales revenues or cash flow? Analyze your fixed costs, as well as your variable costs. Determine how much you would have to pay out in rents, salaries, wages, expenses, and other outlays to keep your doors open. This is your break-even point.

How many months could you survive if your income were cut off for any period of time? You should have a cash reserve of at least three months put aside to prepare for emergencies. Many companies went bankrupt after the terrorist attacks on September 11, 2001, when their business came to a halt for two or three months. They had no reserves available and no way to acquire those reserves during the situation that existed at that time. Don't let this happen to you.

Just as your job is to push forward aggressively to create and keep customers, it is also your responsibility to economize at all times so that you have the necessary resources to survive, no matter what happens. Remember, there are risks that you cannot afford to take, and spending too much on operations, or to achieve a particular goal, is one of those unacceptable risks.

The Principle of Economy and Personal Success

The principle of economy applies to every area of your life. The reason that individuals and organizations want more, sooner, easier, and with greater certainty is because, consciously or unconsciously, they recognize that life is precious and resources are scarce.

You can never do everything you want to do. You can never buy everything you want to buy. You have to choose. And you always have to choose what you feel is going to give you the highest and best return, both in the short term and in the long term. As Patton said of the U.S. troops, "Every battle we fight will result in a gain for us or we will not fight." If this basic principle is ignored, you risk losing valuable resources and losing later.

The Battle of the Kursk Salient

The tank battle in the Kursk salient in the Soviet Union in the summer of 1943 was a decisive battle of World War II and also the largest tank battle that took place in that conflict. Both the Germans and the Soviets threw in all of their tanks and armored vehicles to attack and counterattack. After days of bitter fighting back and forth, the Germans were finally forced to withdraw with the loss of most of their armor. It was the end of German offensives on the Eastern Front. The Germans had 70,000 troops killed or captured and 2,950 tanks and 1400 aircraft destroyed. From that point onward, it was not possible for Germany to win the war.

The Germans had suffered what are called "absolute losses." These are losses that cannot be made up in time. The Soviets had only suffered "relative losses." They had sacrificed a large number of tanks and armored vehicles in this battle, but they were able to manufacture new ones to replace them and continue their advance along the Eastern Front toward Berlin. The Germans also engaged in a tank manufacturing program, but by the time the new German Tiger Tanks came into use, they had been driven back all along the Russian Front. They had lost the Battles of Leningrad, Moscow, and Stalingrad and were unable to regain their previous momentum. The War was lost.

The Principle of Economy and Income

The average income in America is about $25,000 per year for an individual and $36,000 for a family. Your first goal, when you begin your career, is to hit the averages. Your second goal should be to beat the averages by as great a margin as possible.

Some people, over the course of their lifetimes, will see their incomes increase by 3 percent to 5 percent per year, just at or slightly ahead of the rate of inflation, or cost-of-living increases. After twenty, thirty, or forty years of hard work, the average person will be earning the average income for their job and position at that time.

As you become more knowledgeable and experienced at your work, you will become more valuable to your company, and you will receive more than a new person starting out. However, this is not always the case. An engineer graduating from a university today already knows about 80 percent of the material of an engineer who graduated ten years ago. But the new engineer will work for half the salary. If a person graduates in engineering and does not continually upgrade his knowledge and skills, he will quickly be replaced by a new graduate engineer who will work for far less and contribute almost as much.

In a well-publicized case recently, an older executive was laid off by a major corporation and replaced by a younger executive who was willing to work for much less. The older executive sued for *age discrimination*. The court ruled against him. The judge determined that it was not discrimination if the company was able to hire a younger person who could do the same job at a lower price. This was simply a basic economic principle upon which our system is built.

The real problem was that the older executive had been coasting for several years. He had stopped increasing his knowledge and skills years before. He had fallen so far behind that the value of his contribution was no greater than the contribution of a person ten or twenty years younger. This is a phenomenon that we are seeing throughout our competitive market society. It will continue all our lives.

The Definition of a Job

A job is an opportunity to make a contribution to your company that is greater than the amount your company has to pay you to do the job. As long as your contribution is greater than your cost, the company can afford to keep you on. But if you don't keep your knowledge and skills up-to-date, someone who is more ambitious than you and who is willing to make an equal or greater contribution for a lower salary will soon replace you.

When you go into the marketplace as a customer, you always seek to get the very most for the very least. You want the highest quality and quantity of products and services at the lowest possible cost. It is the same way with hiring someone or with a job.

In the world of work, each person views their own work as something unique and special. They view themselves and their labor as something that is different and apart from all other people.

However, the market is *neutral*. In the market, the labor of another person is merely a factor of production. And like any other factor of production, companies that hire people are always looking to get the very most for the very least or at the lowest cost. All things being equal, the company would soon go out of business if it paid more for an employee than it absolutely had to in a competitive economy.

Your job is to make sure that you are worth the kind of money that you want to earn. This is the best "economy" of all.

The Source of High-Paying Jobs

Every employer attempts to economize in the acquisition of the factors of production, including the factor of labor. In reality, a job is a 'Performance Management Agreement' whereby the employee agrees to provide a certain quality and quantity of labor which can be combined with the labor of others to produce a product or service. In every case, because of the Law of Supply and Demand, employers attempt to get the very most of any particular kind of work or result at the very lowest cost.

Not long ago, the then secretary of labor Robert Reich proclaimed that "America must create more high-paying jobs for its workforce."

This is an interesting statement that demonstrates a complete ignorance of basic economics. The first question that should have been asked of Mr. Reich was, "What part of America is responsible for creating these 'high-paying jobs?'"

Is it the mountains or valleys of America that are responsible for creating these jobs? Is it the trees or lakes or minerals under the ground? Is it the rivers or beaches or oceans? Is it some specific individual or group of individuals that is responsible for creating these high-paying jobs? A better question would be "Where do high-paying jobs come from, and who really *creates* a high-paying job?"

When you think about it, you realize immediately that high-paying jobs are created by individuals who make themselves highly productive. It is not possible for anyone *outside* of the individual to create a high-paying job for her. Only you, by continually working on yourself, by continually upgrading your own skills and knowledge, can make yourself more productive and therefore more highly paid in a competitive marketplace. There is no other way.

Increase Your Return on Energy

As an individual, your most precious resource is your time. Your income and your standard of living are determined by how well and how efficiently you sell your time. You must therefore practice the principle of economy in using your time in the very best way possible to assure the highest quality and quantity of results for the efforts that you put in.

The aim of all strategic planning and strategic thinking in business is to increase the *return on equity*. However, your equity in your life is personal. It consists of your physical, mental, and emotional time and energy. Your job in life therefore is to increase your "return on energy." To put it another way, your job is to earn the highest possible "return on life."

People who are earning vastly more than the average person are not necessarily smarter or more talented. But they are willing to do things that the average person is not willing to do. And if you do the same things that the most productive and highest-paid people do, you will soon begin to enjoy the same rewards they do.

If you wanted to earn $100,000 per year, and you had a choice of achieving that income goal in five years or ten years, which would you choose? The answer is obvious. All things being equal, you would prefer to reach a $100,000 income in five years rather than ten years. Whatever your income goal, you want to reach it sooner rather than later. The only question is then "How do you do it?"

Today, time and knowledge are the primary sources of value. Your ability to achieve a result, either for yourself or for someone else, faster than someone else, represents real value. Your ability to attain results will soon be reflected in the amount you earn.

Your ability to use your time effectively to get more done faster, more easily, and with greater certainty, for yourself and others, is the key to economizing on the amount of time and energy you spend achieving your major objectives.

Step on the Accelerator of Your Life

There are nine factors that you can apply to your life to increase the speed at which you achieve your goals, increase your income, and fulfill your potential. Each of these factors is essential in the achievement of great success. When you systematically implement one or more of these factors into your life, you put your foot on the accelerator of your own career and begin moving ahead more rapidly than you perhaps ever thought possible. By getting results faster, you practice the principle of economy in achieving more of your goals with a smaller expenditure of time — your most precious resource.

Learn All You Can. The first "accelerator" is *education*. We live in a knowledge-based society where the highest-paid people are those who know more than others. They know more of the critical facts, ideas, and information than the average person in their field. As a result, they make a more valuable contribution in a knowledge-based society. They are more highly respected and are ultimately paid more money and promoted faster.

Specialized knowledge can be applied to save time, energy, effort, expenditure, and resources. The more knowledgeable you are in a particular area, the faster, easier, and more certain it is that you will get the results that are necessary or expected in that area.

The rule is "To earn more, you must learn more." If you want to increase your level of income, you must increase your level of intellectual capital. You must increase the amount of knowledge you have to apply to what you are doing.

Commit to Excellence. The second accelerator you can develop to achieve your goals faster and easier is *skill*. How well you do your job will largely determine how much you earn. The quality and quantity of your results is the deciding factor in your success. The better you get at what you do, the faster and easier it becomes for you to get the job done in a timely fashion.

If you are in sales, you get better with every sales interaction. Eventually, because of the experience curve, you will be able to make more and more sales in less and less time. You will become more fluent on the telephone. You will become more competent in dealing with people face-to-face. You will become more aware of and sensitive to people's real needs and concerns.

As your skills increase, you will become more skilled at presenting your products or services and answering the questions or concerns that the customer might have. You will become more focused in terms of getting your customer to take action to proceed with your offering. You will become more and more confident getting sales and referrals from your satisfied customers.

If you are a manager, the more you study and practice the essential skills of planning, organizing, staffing, delegating, supervising, measuring, and reporting, the better you get at each one of them. As a result, it will take you less and less time to get more and better results. You will achieve an ever-higher level of outputs with a decreasing level of inputs.

Ben Feldman of New York Life was once rated as the greatest salesman in the world, according to *Guinness World Records.* When he began his sales career in 1942, he resolved to make two sales per week. In his earlier years, these two sales per week were quite small, but over time, as he improved, the size of his sales grew. By the time he reached his peak, he was earning many millions of dollars per year in straight commission sales, even though he was still making only *two* sales per week. Because of his greatly increased knowledge and skill, he was able to make larger and larger sales every time.

Developing your skills and abilities is like climbing a ladder. You cannot skip steps without slipping and falling. You have to take it one step at a time. But you can invest more time in developing your skills. You can increase the speed at which you learn the things you need to know to achieve the goals you want to achieve.

Expand Your Network. Your goal is to accomplish as much as possible in the shortest period of time. One way you can do this is by developing an ever-widening circle of contacts. You will find that almost every major change in your life involves a person or persons who either opens or closes a door for you. Everything in life turns out to be the result of *relationships*. The number of people who know you and like you and who are willing to help you will largely determine your success in any area.

To broaden your network of contacts, you must network continually, at every opportunity. Join your professional associations and get involved with the other people in your field. Attend social and business functions and introduce yourself to other people. Never stop broadening your circle of contacts.

The reason for the relationship between contacts and success is simple. People always prefer to buy from someone they know. They feel more comfortable recommending people they have met, even if it was only once.

Save Your Money. Having money in the bank gives you greater freedom, and the ability to take advantage of opportunities when they come along. If you are broke or in debt, you have very few options open to you. Even if you are presented with a great opportunity, you won't be able to do anything with it.

You are only as free as your options. If you have no options, you have no freedom. If you are stuck in a dead-end job that you cannot leave because you have no money set aside, you have put a brake on your potential. You are locked in place. You can spin your wheels and lose months and years of your time by the very fact that you have no choice but to accept whatever situation you are in.

W. Clement Stone, who started as a 12-year old paperboy and accumulated a fortune of almost a billion dollars, once wrote, "A part of all you earn is yours to keep, and if you cannot save money, the seeds of greatness are not in you."

Get the Job Done Quickly. One of the accelerators that can help you as much as anything else is a reputation for good work habits. Your ability to increase your ROTI or "return on time invested," can enable you to accomplish vastly more in a shorter period of time than another person who is disorganized and inefficient.

The basic formula for high performance is "E x E = R" or "Effectiveness x Efficiency = Results." "Effectiveness" means doing the right things. "Efficiency" means doing them right. Effectiveness and efficiency both require that you set goals, analyze your work carefully, determine your priorities, and always focus on the highest-value use of your time.

The development of good work habits requires that you think before acting. Make a list of everything you have to do before you begin. Set careful priorities on the list before you start on your first task. Good work habits require that you consider the likely consequences, positive or negative, of what you do. Becoming highly productive requires that you continually ask, "What is the most valuable use of my time right now?" And whatever your answer to this question, work on that task exclusively.

A Positive Mental Attitude. One of the most important factors in career success is a positive mental attitude. Your attitude is very much a decision that you make. Regardless of your previous experiences or your background, you can become more positive by practicing many of the techniques that we have talked about in this book. Not only do you "become what you think about," but you "become what you do" as well. If you engage in the same activities that positive, confident, optimistic people engage in, you will eventually feel and act the way they do.

A positive mental attitude has best been defined as "a positive response to stress." Your life will be a continuous series of problems and difficulties, successes and failures, triumphs and disappointments. Since these ups and downs are unavoidable and inevitable, the only part that you can control is the way that you respond. This is the key to a positive mental attitude.

Anyone can remain positive when things are going well. It is when you have problems and difficulties that you demonstrate what you are *really* made of. Your ability to find something positive in every situation is what enables you to see the positive aspects of the situation. When you focus on the solution rather than the problem, you remain optimistic. You manufacture your own positive attitude by choosing what you will think about. You take complete control over your emotions.

Look the Part. Just as a positive attitude will help you more than any other factor in your relationships, a positive image will open many doors for you as well. People judge you by the way you look on the outside. You may not like this, but it just so happens that you judge everyone else by the way they look on the outside as well. When you present an attractive image in your person, your clothing, your grooming, and your accessories, you will have a positive impact on the people around you. They will be more willing to open doors for you and make opportunities available to you.

People are highly visual in their assessments of others. Most people pass judgment on a new person in the first *four seconds.* They finalize and firm up their initial judgment within thirty seconds of the first contact. People take one glance at you and decide who you really are. From that point on, they seek ways to justify what they have already decided to believe.

When the first impression you make is positive, people tend to see you, hear you, and relate to you in a positive way forever after. If your first impression is negative, they tend to see and hear you in a negative way from that point forward.

Get a book, take a course, and visit a consultant if necessary to make sure you look the part of a successful person. Do whatever is necessary to learn how to present the very best image possible in every situation.

Dress for success. Don't listen to people who tell you that you can dress any way you want in our new casual society. Only people who have a limited future are indifferent to the way they appear to others in a competitive business environment.

Unlock Your Inborn Creativity. Ideas are the keys to the future. One good idea, at the right time and place, can change your entire career. One insight that leads to a breakthrough in your business can put you onto the fast track.

Fortunately, everyone has untapped creative abilities. Creativity is like a muscle. But if you don't use it, you lose it, at least temporarily. The more you practice your creativity, the more creative you become. And in business, creativity is best expressed in your continual seeking for better, faster, easier, cheaper ways to get the job done. One good idea is all you need to start a fortune.

To Have More, You Must Be More. Your reputation for honesty and integrity and the quality of your character will do as much to assure your success as any other factor. The development of a good character is one of the best ways to guarantee that you will progress more rapidly toward the accomplishment of your career goals.

Self-discipline combined with honesty will open countless doors for you. Trust is the foundation of all relationships. When people feel that they can trust you to keep your word and to do what you say you will do, they will give you greater responsibilities. When people feel that they will be more successful getting the things they want by relying on you, they will open countless doors for you.

The Principle of Economy Revisited

Economy in military terms means never spending more men and matériel than is necessary to achieve a particular objective. Economy in business means that you achieve business goals at the lowest possible expenditure of time and resources. Economy in your personal life means organizing your activities so that you achieve more and more of the things you want and need at a lower and lower cost in terms of time and energy.

The principle of economy requires that you continually think about how you can get the highest and best return on your investment of time, energy, and emotion in everything you do. The principle of economy requires that you see yourself as a valuable and unique person whose life is extremely precious. You never spend more of your wonderful life than you need to in order to get the things that matter the most to you. You deploy your resources, your abilities, and your energies skillfully. You make yourself unstoppable.

CHAPTER ELEVEN

The Principle of Surprise
Do the Unexpected

Never attack where the enemy expects you to come.

—GENERAL GEORGE S. PATTON

S peed and deception are critical elements of victory in warfare and in competitive business. If your adversary knows what you are going to do, he can move to counter your efforts and even defeat you by turning the tables. By moving quickly and in complete secrecy, you can gain tremendous advantage and win great battles.

The Inchon Landing

On June 25, 1950, the North Korean People's Army, numbering 100,000 well-armed troops, invaded South Korea in a surprise attack that sent the allies reeling back down the Korean Peninsula and forced them into a small enclave around the city of Pusan. This offensive by North Korea conquered three-quarters of South Korea, destroyed half of the South Korean army and largely demoralized the American and Korean forces.

However, one military surprise triggered another. The North Koreans did not count on the military brilliance of General Douglas MacArthur. Against considerable odds and tremendous resistance from other commanders, McArthur organized on September 15,1950, a seaborne invasion at Inchon well behind the North Korean forces, aimed at cutting the North Korean supply lines and taking back the offensive.

The landing was a brilliant success. Within a few days, it had accomplished all of its objectives. The North Koreans, taken completely by surprise, were cut off and quickly disintegrated as a fighting force. The war went on for two-and-a-half more years before ending at essentially the same place it had begun. But the surprise attack of the Inchon landing was the decisive turning point of what had initially appeared to be an American defeat.

THE PRINCIPLE OF SURPRISE:
Accomplish your purpose before your enemy can react effectively.

Surprise is a most effective and powerful weapon in war, and it can decisively shift the balance of combat power. With surprise, success out of proportion to the energy exerted can be achieved. Surprise results from striking the enemy at a time and place for which he is not fully prepared. Speed, cover, deception, effective intelligence, effective counterintelligence, variations in tactics, and variations in methods of operation are some of the factors that contribute to the game of surprise. Surprise is an absolutely indispensable principle of victory in warfare. If the actions of the attacking commander are not conducted in complete secrecy, the opposing commander will anticipate where the attack is going to occur and prepare against it, often turning the tables on the attacker.

The Principle of Surprise in Business

In your business and your career, surprise is an important tactic that you can use to achieve competitive advantage in rapidly changing markets. Surprise in business today can be summarized in one word, "speed." The elements of speed, deception, and surprise are so important to the successful conduct of military operations that most wars begin with a surprise attack, only followed later by a formal declaration of war.

The first major war of the 20th century, the Russo/Japanese War, opened with a sneak attack by Japanese ships on the Russian fleet anchored off Port Arthur in China on the night of February 8–9, 1904. War was officially declared two days later.

Five Japanese divisions landed above Port Arthur on May 5 to attack the Russian defenses on the heights of Nanhan. Soon the Japanese had more than 80,000 men surrounding Port Arthur, which was defended by less than 42,000 soldiers.

The battle took seven months but finally, on January 2, 1905, the Russians surrendered Port Arthur to the Japanese. The Russian defeat in this war was a direct result of the element of surprise achieved by the Japanese in their initial assault on the Russian fleet in Port Arthur. "Everything which the enemy least expects will succeed the best." (Frederick the Great).

Sun Tzu wrote, "Rapidity is the essence of war; take advantage of the enemy's unreadiness, make your way by unexpected routes, and attack unguarded spots."

The Attack on Pearl Harbor

One of the most devastating surprise attacks in history took place on December 7, 1941 at Pearl Harbor, Hawaii, the advanced base for the U.S. Pacific Fleet.

The military historian John Prados wrote, "Pearl Harbor represented the largest mass use of aircraft carriers up to that time, the furthest-range conduct of a naval attack, the largest air attack against a naval target up to that time, and one of the most elaborate efforts to coordinate simultaneous attacks by aircraft and submarines."

The Japanese strike hit soon after dawn. Eighteen American warships were sunk or damaged. More than 2,400 Americans died and 188 aircraft were destroyed. The successful use of the elements of surprise, speed, and deception by the Japanese at Pearl Harbor are still studied today.

The customer's appetite for speed today is insatiable. Customers want both instantaneous and simultaneous gratification. In fact, for most customers today, instant gratification is no longer *fast* enough. Often the customer, who did not even know that he wanted your product or service until today, now wants it yesterday.

Loyalty today is won by dynamically serving your customer better and faster than anyone else can do it. Your job is to satisfy your customers in "real time." Real time means *immediately*. It means now, at this moment. It means without hesitation.

Real time service is the key to winning and keeping customers. Real time is the shortest possible interval between the idea and the action. Your motto, in dealing with your customers, for the rest of your career should be, "Sure, right away!"

Customers love individuals and organizations that do things for them fast. Whenever your customer has a problem or question of any kind, you respond by saying, "Sure, right away!" These words are music to your customer's ears. Even if you cannot actually do something immediately, you can assure the customer that you have heard her question or need, and that you are taking action without delay.

The Currency of the 21st Century

Time is the currency of the 21st century. Every management breakthrough or new business idea is aimed at reducing the amount of time it takes to achieve a goal or accomplish a particular result. And whatever got you to where you are today, won't keep you there. However quickly you served your customers in the past, you must be serving them even faster and better in the months ahead.

Every day, in every way, you must be continually asking, "How can we serve our customers better and faster than our competitors, and better and faster than they have been served in the past?"

Each new speed record that you set becomes the starting point or benchmark for the next speed record that you must aim at. You can never relax because your competition never does.

The good news is that you can dramatically increase the speed at which you respond to customer needs. There are two keys: First of all, decide to pick up your speed of serving your customers. Second, use your ability to think more creatively about what your customers need and how you can give it to them. Customers appreciate this creative approach more than you can imagine.

Building Customer Loyalty

No matter how good your product or service is today, there are going to be problems with it. It will not work the way it is supposed to work. It will break down. It will give rise to unexpected problems and frustrations on the part of your customer.

Because of these unavoidable product or service problems, your customers will *complain*. This complaining is actually a good sign. The worst customer of all is the dissatisfied customer who does not complain but instead goes somewhere else. If you have too many of these, it can sink your business.

John D. Wanamaker who founded the first great department store in Chicago, once said, "The most expensive customer of all is the one who, though dissatisfied, walks away without saying anything, and never comes back."

In a Harvard study, they found that fully 58% of customers who change suppliers said that they did so because of *indifference* or lack of caring on the part of someone in the company. They didn't complain; they just took their business elsewhere. Dissatisfied customers tell an average of twelve to twenty other people about you. This is the worst advertising you can have.

However, when you respond *quickly* to customer complaints, you actually build greater customer loyalty than before. You increase the likelihood that the customer will buy from you again and recommend you to his friends. Satisfied customers tell an average of five to eight other people about their experience with you. This is the best advertising you can have.

Customers are not unreasonable. They expect to have problems and challenges. The only part of this "challenge-response" situation that you can control is how you respond when a customer has a problem of some kind. When you respond quickly, politely, efficiently, and effectively, customers appreciate you even *more* than customers who have never had a reason to complain in the first place.

Fergal Quinn founded and built the immensely successful Quinn Grocery Store chain throughout Ireland. He explains that one of the keys to his success was his careful analysis of customer complaints. He found that very often, a customer complaint revealed either a new market opportunity, or a problem that could be resolved to increase customer loyalty and attract additional business.

Complaints are often an indication of the ways that you must change your products or services to make them even more attractive to your customers. The insights that come from customer comments and complaints can point you toward terrific ways to increase sales and profitability. For this reason, the best companies use every feedback mechanism possible to solicit complaints and suggestions from their customers. Microsoft Corporation gets fully 80% of its new product ideas from customer feedback.

Ask for Customer Feedback

Hewlett Packard has become one of the most successful hi-tech companies in the world as the result of its virtual obsession with eliciting customer evaluations and responses. HP sends out customer comment cards, conducts customer telephone surveys and meets with customers both individually and in focus groups to find out in depth exactly how they think and feel about their product.

The developers at Hewlett Packard then take these customer comments and suggestions back to the factory and use them as the basis for product improvements. They incorporate them into new research and development activities. As a result, they continually produce high quality products that even more customers want and will pay for.

Change Is the Only Constant

In the turbulent and fast changing markets of today, change is the only constant. Continuous change is inevitable, unpredictable, and discontinuous. Whatever products or services you are offering today, they are already becoming obsolete. Whatever works will stop working, and far sooner than you expect.

For you to ride the wave of change, and stay ahead of the curve, you always have to be thinking about your next move. You must always be looking for ways to make your products and services even better than they are today, even if you are currently the market leader. You can never afford to rest on your laurels, or to become complacent.

One of the best business strategies, even if you are number one in your market, is to always act as if you are number two. The best companies treat their customers every day as if they were on the verge of losing every one of them. They never take them for granted. They remain hypersensitive to the wants and needs of their customers, and they react quickly to any customer problem. The best companies know that the business of tomorrow is built today on a foundation of highly satisfied customers.

Get Out of the Office

More and more companies are insisting that their managers and executives get out into the field, face to face with real, live customers, and listen to them when they talk. The best military commanders are always going into the field, up to the front lines, to personally see and experience what their men are facing. By the same token, the best managers regularly go out with their salespeople to meet with customers and find out exactly how customers are reacting and responding to their product and service offerings.

One of the great executives of the 20th century was Alfred P. Sloan, the head of General Motors for many years, and the man most responsible for making it the largest industrial corporation in the world. Alfred P. Sloan used to take one day off each month during which he would put on a sports coat and work in a General Motors dealership as a salesman. He would meet and talk with customers and get their opinions on GM cars and service firsthand.

Many airlines today insist that their executives spend one day each month checking in passengers and baggage down in the terminal so that they have a feeling for how their customers are being treated, and how they are reacting to that treatment.

At Ford Motor Corporation, many executives are required to work on the complaint desk, fielding phone calls from customers, for one day a month. This gives them a chance to ask questions and get timely feedback that is usually unavailable from any other source.

Israeli-Arab War

The 1967 war was the third war between Israel and its Arab neighbors since the formation of the State of Israel in 1948. Despite having been defeated in 1948–1949 and again in 1956, Egypt, Jordan, and Syria had continued to steadily build up their military forces for another attack on Israel.

On the morning of June 5, 1967, Israeli planes launched a massive surprise attack on Egyptian, Jordanian, and Syrian airfields, destroying 374 enemy aircraft, most still on the ground.

With complete air superiority, Israeli armored columns drove into the Gaza Strip, and spread westward into the Sinai Peninsula in a three-pronged advance toward the Suez Canal. Within three days of fighting, the Egyptian Army was in flight on all fronts. Egypt lost Sinai and the Gaza strip.

Meanwhile, Israeli forces occupied the Old City of Jerusalem and the West Bank on June 7 and Jordan surrendered. Syria surrendered on June 10, having lost the Golan Heights to Israel. The war cost the lives of many thousands of Arab soldiers and civilians, and 679 Israeli soldiers.

This Six-Day War was a brilliant example of the use of speed and surprise against a superior enemy, serving as a "Force Multiplier" for the Israelis, and enabling them to achieve victory against overwhelming odds.

In business, the ability to marshal all of your resources and take rapid action in a way completely unexpected by your competition can give you a market advantage. As Von Clausewitz said, "The two factors that produce surprise are secrecy and speed." You must use these yourself at every opportunity to achieve and maintain meaningful competitive advantage for your business.

Meaningful Competitive Advantage

The key to business success is for you to achieve meaningful competitive advantage. As an entrepreneur, one of the advantages you can gain over your larger competitors is speed and personalization. Large companies are more likely to take customers for granted than small companies. For a small company, a single customer represents a far greater percentage of business than that same customer would represent for a larger company. Often, people will deal with you for no other reason than that you promise to satisfy them faster than anyone else. Your small size can actually be an advantage for your customer.

In this sense, *speed* can be your differentiating factor, your competitive advantage. Customers will pay a premium for speed. Often they will forego product or service quality as long as they can have it immediately. Just look at the multi-billion dollar success of fast food throughout the United States and throughout the world.

A Billion Dollars From Fast Delivery

Tom Monahan was a young man delivering pizzas at the University of Michigan in East Lansing when he made an important discovery. A customer would phone in and order a pizza. The order would be received, the pizza would be made by hand, baked, and boxed, and then he would deliver it about an hour after the order had been received. However, when he arrived with the pizza, most of his customers were impatient and angry. They hardly appreciated that the pizza was being delivered to their door. They just complained about how long it took to get a pizza once they had ordered it.

Tom Monahan had an insight that made him one of the richest men in the world, worth more than 1.8 billion dollars. It dawned on him, like a light bulb going off, that when people ordered a pizza, they were hungry, *right now*. And when they were hungry, speed was more important than quality.

He asked the people he was working for if there wasn't some way that they could speed up pizza delivery. They told him that it was impossible to do it any faster. A pizza took a certain amount of time to prepare, especially with 30 different combinations and ingredients. They could not be made and delivered in less than an hour.

Tom Monahan decided that he could do it better. He sold his used car, rented a bankrupt pizza parlor with a pizza oven and began offering a limited number of the most popular pizzas, based on his experience. He promised delivery within 30 minutes or no charge. In no time at all, Dominos Pizza took off. It became one of the most successful fast food franchises in the history of the industry.

Do It Faster, Better, Cheaper

Look at your business. Study it carefully. What is it that you could do right now to increase the speed at which you serve your customers with exactly what they want and need and are willing to pay for?

One of the most important areas for developing speed and creativity in business is called "line-of-sight theory." This theory states that, in your *line of sight*, in your current job, right where you are, right now, you can always see little things that you can do to reduce the amount of time that it takes to accomplish a particular result.

Sometimes, this improvement can be as simple as answering the telephone within two rings and taking action immediately on any customer question or complaint. Sometimes, you can increase your speed by organizing everything you need before the workday begins so that you can respond instantly when the customer calls.

The IBM Story

IBM had a challenge some years ago. An IBM salesman would sell a computer system to a company and offer to finance it through the IBM Finance Corporation. But it was taking 6–8 weeks for IBM to process the application and get back to the customer with an approval, or disapproval. Upon investigation, IBM found that fully fourteen different people worked in the IBM Credit Approval Department reviewing customer applications prior to issuing an approval or disapproval.

IBM decided to reengineer the process to speed up the approval process. Using their own internal resources, they computerized the entire program. They soon found that fully 95% of credit applications could be approved or disapproved immediately. Only 5% required further investigation.

Not only that, they found that if the IBM sales representative filled out the necessary information on an application form on her laptop computer, the application could be sent by modem to the head office and processed immediately. As a result of these improvements, they reduced the time of approval for a credit application from six weeks to two hours, and sometimes, to a few minutes. An IBM rep could make the sale in the morning, the credit application would arrive by noon and the customer could receive approval before the day was out. This speed-up in the credit approval process increased sales dramatically and almost immediately.

The Power of Focus

A problem with many companies today is that they have too many products and services, in too many combinations, at too many price points, being offered to too many customers in too many markets. If clarity is the key to success in business and in life, fuzziness or lack of focus is a major reason for failure and frustration. The greater the number of product or service offerings there are, the longer it takes to make a sale and to satisfy a customer with what he or she wants and needs right now.

You incorporate the element of surprise and speed into your business by deciding upon the one or two things that you can do that customers will appreciate more than anything else. Decide today to make speed your competitive advantage. Remember, if you have the very best product or service in your marketplace but it takes too long for your customer to get it, you will lose sale after sale to faster moving competitors. Be continually looking for faster, newer, better, and easier ways to sell and deliver your products and services so that your customers will choose to deal with you rather than with anyone else.

The Customer Is Always Right

Peter Drucker has written, "The purpose of a business is to satisfy customers." This means that the customer is always right. Whatever the customer wants, the customer gets. Your job is to find out what your customers really want, need, and are willing to pay for and then to give it to them, faster than anyone else.

There are *four* levels of customer service that are possible in your business. Reaching each of these levels is like climbing a ladder. You rise to the next level by mastering the previous level.

1. Customer Satisfaction. You achieve customer satisfaction when you satisfy your customer's basic wants and needs in such a way that your customer has no real complaints. You meet their expectations. This is the *minimum* level necessary to survive in business today. The sad fact is that many companies and individuals think that "customer satisfaction" is the high point of achievement when it is really just a minimum condition to stay in business.

2. Exceed Customer Expectations. The second level of customer satisfaction is when you exceed customer expectations. This is the basic requirement for *growth* in your business. One of the great success principles is: "Your success will always be in direct proportion to what you do for your customers *after* you do what they expect you to do."

If you only do what you are expected to do, you are in an extremely tenuous position. You are setting yourself up to be knocked off by anyone who comes along and does more than you are currently doing. It is when you do more than is expected that you start to pull ahead of your competitors.

3. Delight Your Customers. The third level of customer service is when you do vastly more than just meet or exceed customer expectations. Companies like Nordstrom have developed a national reputation for delighting their customers with the quality of service that they give to each person. Almost everyone who shops at Nordstrom has a "Nordstrom" story of some kind that they eagerly share with others. These Nordstrom stories are really word-of-mouth advertising testimonials to keep people going back to Nordstrom's and cause new people to shop there.

Here is my Nordstrom story: When my son David was seven years old, he came home one evening and said that he had to appear in a school play the next day with black stovepipe trousers and a white shirt. Typically, he had known this for some time but had forgotten to tell us. By the time he mentioned it, it was already 8 o'clock at night, and David did not have the trousers that he needed. He was upset and worried. He felt that he was going to be embarrassed and would look silly if he didn't have the proper clothes. I was out of town, and my wife could not leave the house and go shopping because we had small children. What could she do?

Barbara immediately phoned her "personal shopper" at Nordstrom and explained the dilemma. The Nordstrom saleswoman said that she would go down to the boys' department and pick up three pairs of pants in the size that Barbara requested. She would then drop them off at our house on the way home. Barbara could then take back the pants she didn't need at a later date.

Our home is about thirty minutes north of the Nordstrom store in San Diego. At about 9:30 P.M., when David was already asleep, the Nordstrom saleswoman arrived at the door with three pairs of pants. She filled out the charge slip and went on her way.

The next morning, when David woke up, he had three pairs of brand new trousers to choose from. One of the pairs of pants fit him perfectly. He went off to his school play absolutely delighted and convinced that his mother could work miracles.

Now, here is the *rest* of the story. When Barbara took the unneeded pairs of pants back to Nordstrom, she spoke to the saleswoman and found that the saleswoman lived thirty minutes *south* of the Nordstrom store. She had driven half an hour north to drop off the pants and had then had to drive one hour south to get home that night. She had gone completely out of her way not only to meet expectations and to exceed expectations, but to absolutely *delight* her customer. This is the kind of customer service behavior that generates loyalty that goes far beyond the price shopping that characterizes most purchase activities.

4. Amaze Your Customers. This is the highest level of all in customer service. You amaze your customers when you do things for them similar to what the saleswoman did for us when David needed pants for the next day. Delighting your customers leaves your customer shaking her head in amazement.

There are several Platinum cards offered by the various credit card companies. They cost far more than a regular credit card and entitle the holder to special services. *Fortune* did a report on the benefits of the various offerings and overwhelmingly recommended the American Express Platinum Card.

The article recounted the story of an American Platinum Card holder who had a heart attack while on vacation in Mexico. It was extremely serious, and the Mexican hospital was not set up to give him the emergency care he required to save his life. They called American Express for help.

Because emergency medical service was included with his Platinum Card, American Express immediately commissioned a private jet to fly into Mexico with a heart specialist on board and evacuate the patient immediately. They rushed him into surgery in a top American hospital and saved his life. The total bill was over $50,000. American Express paid it all under the provisions of the Platinum Card. *That* is superb customer service!

Remember, your success in life will be in direct proportion to what you do *after* you do what you are expected to do. Your aim is to always do more than you are paid for. Your goal should always be to go *the extra mile*. There are never any traffic jams on the extra mile.

You should study every aspect of your business and your customer relations activities, continually seeking ways to greatly exceed customer expectations and then to delight and amaze the people you depend upon for your success.

Satisfy Your Most Important Customer

When I began my career as a young executive, I recognized very early on that my success was going to be largely determined by how well I satisfied my primary customer, my *boss*. I therefore made a decision that, whatever my boss asked for, I would do it fast. This decision marked a turning point in my life. It transformed my career.

Whatever he asked me to do, I did it immediately, even if I had to work all weekend to finish something he had only asked me for on Friday afternoon.

Within a few months, I had a reputation with him for being the person he gave the job to if he wanted it done quickly and well. Within a year, I had my own department. In two years, I was running three departments with large projects in three countries. I went far beyond every other executive in that company, primarily because I moved quickly whenever anything needed to be done.

When you also develop a reputation for doing things quickly and well, you will get more and better opportunities to do even more things faster and better. And the more opportunities you have to use your skills and abilities, the better you will get, and the more opportunities you will be given.

Focus on Solutions

The purpose of a business is to create and keep a customer. How do you create and keep customers? One way is to think continually in terms of what your product or service *does* to improve the life or work of your customers and then continually look for ways to do that better. All products and services are actually solutions to problems or means to the satisfaction of customers' needs. A product or service is merely a way to achieve a particular goal for your customer. It is not what your product or service *is*, but only what it *does* for your customer that moves him to buy.

Identify the biggest single complaint or dissatisfaction that your product or service can resolve for your customers. What is the critical need they have that your product satisfies? What is the biggest problem they have that your product solves? What is the most important goal that your product or service helps them to achieve? Focus all your energies on the answers to these questions, and take action quickly. Your creative solution and the speed with which you fixed the problem will surprise your customers.

Reposition Yourself in the Market

There are thousands of companies throughout the United States that perform housecleaning services for working families. But Merry Maids has become a $500-million-dollar giant in the home housecleaning industry. How did they do it? They repositioned themselves against their competition!

While most companies were selling housecleaning services, usually on the basis of price, Merry Maids repositioned themselves as something else. They did something different. Rather than selling housecleaning services, they positioned themselves as "Sellers of Leisure Time."

Instead of offering to come in and clean the house better than their competitors, they offered to save homeowners several hours of weekend time that they would normally spend doing the housekeeping that had piled up during the week. For a few dollars on a Thursday or Friday, a couple or a family could have an entire weekend free from the nitty-gritty concerns of household maintenance.

While people might have been uncertain or unsure about paying for housecleaning services, most people had no problem at all buying extra "leisure time." This repositioning set Merry Maids so far apart from their competition that they went on to dominate the market.

How could you reposition your product or service in such a way that it satisfies a deep underlying need or problem for your customers? How could you better focus on what your product or service does rather than what it is? How can you surprise your customer into paying attention and noticing your product? This is the key to repositioning yourself.

Always Ask for Feedback

When you meet with your customers, always ask the question "How can we improve our services to you?"

Always ask them how you can serve them better *next time*. The rule is that, if customers do not complain, it often means that they are dissatisfied and thinking of going somewhere else. A complaining customer is a good customer, as long as you take fast action on the complaint.

Many companies make the common mistake of soliciting feedback by asking a question like, "How are we doing?" or "Is everything OK?"

But the fact is that customers don't want to fight with you or get into an argument. When you ask them a bland question like, "How is it going?" they will simply reply by saying, "Fine."

But when you ask, "How can we do it better next time?" almost every customer will give you feedback and ideas that, if you act upon them, can give you and your company an edge in the industry.

Another question you can ask is, "How would we have to change, or what would we have to do differently, to get more of your business?"

Customers today prefer to purchase from a single supplier. They prefer to work with a single firm that understands their special needs and that can be depended upon to provide them with a consistently high level of product or service quality.

At the same time, more vendors and suppliers are focusing on depth of customer rather than breadth of market. Keep asking your customers, "What would we have to do to get 100 percent of your business? What would we have to change, improve, add, take away, or do differently in order to be the preferred provider in our market?"

Ask the Right Questions

A wonderful statement/question that you can use to get ideas for innovation and improvement in your product or service offerings is this: "Mr. Customer, no product or service is perfect, including this one. What weaknesses do you see in our products and services, and how could we make them better in the future?"

When customers are honestly asked for their ideas and opinions, and when you then take action on those ideas and suggestions, your customers become more loyal and determined to buy from you again in the future.

Your Competition Determines Your Strategy

In business, as in warfare, all strategy is formulated with reference to competitors, to the opposing side. It is not possible for you to sit and formulate a marketing strategy alone in a room. You must always be thinking about who you are competing against and what you can do to achieve superiority over them.

The elements of speed and surprise are only possible by thoroughly understanding your opposition and what they are most likely to think and do.

Analyze your major and minor competitors. Who are they? What are their major strengths? Why do customers prefer to buy from your competitors rather than buying from you? You can't hit a target you can't see. You can't achieve superiority in your market if you are not clear about why it is that you are not already superior.

Admire Your Best Competitors

Many people make the mistake of criticizing their successful competitors. But this policy is not helpful. It doesn't teach you anything. You should instead admire them and look for ways to learn from them. Study what they do and respect them for their successes. Admiration and respect are the starting point of emulation, and emulation is the starting point of overtaking.

Once you have identified who they are and what they are doing better than you, you can decide how you are going to beat them. You determine how to change your offerings or methods of doing business. You emphasis your strengths and look for ways to capitalize on their vulnerabilities. You figure out how to use the element of surprise to both capture the attention of the customer and catch the competition off guard.

The Invasion of Normandy

In 1944, in World War II, the Allies created a nonexistent army in southern England with General George S. Patton in command. Phony radio traffic gave the impression of thousands of men being prepared for a cross-channel invasion at the Pas de Calais in France. In response, the Germans massed their infantry and tanks to resist the attack, which never came.

In one of the most remarkable surprise attacks in history, the Allied armies under the command of General Dwight D. Eisenhower attacked instead along the beaches of Normandy, moving hundreds of ships and thousands of men under cover of night. Although the resistance was stiff and the fighting was fierce, the Allies took the beaches relatively quickly, and the Germans were caught completely off guard.

So effective were the creative deception and the surprise attack at Normandy that the Germans were initially convinced that it was merely a diversionary tactic. They made the fatal mistake of holding their main panzer divisions and forces in reserve at Calais waiting for the "real invasion," which never came. By the time they realized the truth, the Allies had secured the beaches. The war was over eleven months later.

Use Your Creativity

Once upon a time, there was a small furniture retailer in a large city who suddenly found himself squeezed between two giant multistory furniture stores going up on either side of his small building. These companies had vastly more resources and a greater selection of furniture at discount prices. The two companies raced to finish their stores, and both held their grand openings in the same week.

He knew he could not compete with their huge advertising budgets for radio, television, and newspaper, so he decided to use his creativity instead. With the huge furniture stores on either side of his building, right above his front doors, he put up a large sign that said "Main Entrance."

What can you do to counter the strengths of your competitors? How can you use deception, surprise, speed, and maneuver to create perceptions of unique added value in the minds of your customers? What can you do to offset the perceived competitive advantage of the companies that are outselling you in the market today?

Look at Yourself Honestly

Success in a competitive market is only possible when you introduce product or service innovations in a way, and at a time and place, that your competition does not expect. To plan, prepare, and use surprise, deception, and speed effectively to achieve business success, you must continually reevaluate and review your offerings and your activities relative to what other companies are doing in the same market.

Be completely honest with yourself. What are your major weaknesses or vulnerabilities relative to your competitors? Remember, no product or service is perfect, including yours. Where do you get the greatest number of complaints? What reasons do your customers give you for not buying your product or service today? And most importantly, what could you do to offset or neutralize your vulnerabilities?

Practice this exercise regularly. Complete the sentence: "We could sell twice as much if it weren't for . . ."

Write down every reason or objection that your customers give you for not buying more of your products or services or for buying from your competitors instead of you. What could you do to neutralize, minimize, or downplay your competitors' strengths or to compensate for your own vulnerabilities?

An excellent exercise you can practice is to imagine that you were starting your business or your sales career over again today. If you could create your business or sales career exactly the way you wanted it, without any obstacles or limitations, what would it look like?

Define your *ideal* customers. What would you have to do to get more of them? How would you have to change your product or service offerings so that you could dominate your market? What additional markets could you go into? What additional distribution channels could you use? How could you change or modify your product or service offerings to make them more attractive to more people?

The Principle of Surprise in Personal Success

The more you do of what you are doing, the more you will get of what you have got. Do the unexpected. Sometimes the most effective thing you can do is exactly the opposite of what you have been doing up until now.

Take the initiative to develop new knowledge and new skills that enable you to make a more valuable contribution to your company. Make suggestions for change and volunteer for additional assignments. Consider changing jobs, or even getting into an entirely new line of work. Be prepared to move across the country to start a new and different career in a different field.

The greatest enemy of success is complacency. This happens when you slip into a comfort zone at your work or in your personal life. You become comfortable and content doing your job and living your life the same old way, even if you are no longer enjoying the fulfillment and satisfaction that you once did. When you begin to feel bored or unchallenged, often it is time for you to do something surprising or unexpected.

Whatever problems or difficulties you are facing in your life today, think about solving them in completely new and different ways. Imagine starting over. What would you do differently? Imagine that you had no limitations of time, money, or resources. What would you get into, or out of?

The only constant today is change. And with regard to change, you have two choices. You can either take the initiative and make the changes you need to make to enjoy the kind of life you desire, or you can wait until the changes are forced upon you by other people and circumstances.

The greatest enemies of human success have always been the fears of failure and rejection. The foundations of personal performance have always been courage and confidence. What would you dare to dream if you knew you could not fail? Whatever you would really like to be, have, or do, set it as a goal, make a plan, and then work on it every day. Be prepared to do the unexpected. You may be surprised at the incredible results you get.

The Principle of Surprise Revisited

The answers to these questions are never final. And there are no answers that are guaranteed to work every time. Your job is to incorporate the principle of surprise, combined with creativity and innovation, into everything you do in your business and personal life.

CHAPTER TWELVE

The Principle of Exploitation

Follow Up and Follow Through

Victory belongs to the most persevering.

—NAPOLEON BONAPART

Throughout history, great battles have been won and then lost because of the failure of a commanding general to follow through and complete the victory.

The Battle for the Dardanelles

In 1915, the British fleet attempted to send a force into the Dardanelles, invade Turkey, which was allied with Germany, and capture the capital city, which at the time was Constantinople. The British battleships entered the strait and bombarded the Turkish positions on the heights for several days while the Turks fired back with all the artillery at their disposal.

But the Turkish gunners were running out of ammunition. British victory seemed inevitable. Reportedly, the order came down from the Turkish government to the army to break off the attack and surrender to the British at 12 o'clock noon, thereby turning the Gallipoli Peninsula over to the British forces.

At the critical moment, 11:00 A.M., within reach of victory, but unaware that they had almost won the battle, the British called off the bombardment. This failure to follow through just one hour longer cost them the battle.

The Gallipoli Campaign

Having been unsuccessful in their naval assault, the British decided to attack Turkey by land. Along with soldiers from Australia and New Zealand, British troops launched a land invasion to seize the Gallipoli Peninsula at the mouth of the Dardanelles. Their attack was a complete surprise, and the Turkish army was caught unprepared. The British were able to land practically unopposed, unloading thousands of fresh troops onto the beaches within a few hours.

But once again, the British hesitated. The commander was cautious. He decided to wait until the entire army was disembarked and ready for action. The Turks, meanwhile, rushed every available soldier, machine gun, and piece of artillery to the heights above the beaches. By the time the British decided to move to assault the heights, it was too late. The Turks were ready and waiting.

The failure to follow through speedily after landing resulted in the legendary disaster known as the Gallipoli Campaign, which cost the British and their allies 100,000 men, and which ultimately failed. The failure to carry through with the naval bombardment, combined with the failure to carry through on the ground, led to one of the greatest military debacles of the twentieth century.

THE PRINCIPLE OF EXPLOITATION:
Follow up and follow through vigorously on a break-through or advantage, once it's achieved.

Keep the enemy off balance. Never allow your opponent the opportunity to regroup and defend or counterattack. Press your advantage and push through to complete victory. Never relax until your objective has been attained.

There are countless examples in military history and business where the failure to follow up and follow through led to the complete loss of everything already won at such a cost in time and resources.

The Principle of Exploitation Applied to Business

It is amazing how many companies come up with innovations and breakthroughs in products and services and then put them aside or fail to exploit them fully in a competitive market. They are then astonished when rival companies emerge into the market with similar ideas and leapfrog them and the rest of the competition to take a commanding lead in customer service and satisfaction. For example, in 1960, the Swiss Chronological Institute in Geneva developed the first quartz watch. At that time, there were 62,500 professional Swiss watchmakers, and Swiss watches were the most popular and highly respected watches in the world. When the Swiss Chronological Institute developed the quartz watch, traditional Swiss watch makers dismissed it as a novelty that had no commercial application. After all, Swiss watchmakers claimed, it lacked the sophisticated internal workings of gears, springs, stems, and other mechanical parts that everyone "knew" had to be included in a watch. Who would be interested in a watch mechanism made of quartz, with virtually no moving parts?

Representatives of a Japanese company visited the Swiss Chronological Institute and were shown the new watch. They saw its potential and offered to purchase the rights from the Swiss Chronological Institute. Believing that its invention was worthless, the Institute sold it to the Japanese company for a small royalty.

The Japanese company had seen something the Swiss hadn't: an opportunity to manufacture watches that were highly accurate and inexpensive as well as attractive. Within a few years, they were mass producing quartz watches and selling them worldwide at a fraction of what the Swiss watchmakers were charging. Within a decade, the Swiss watch industry had been decimated. The number of Swiss watchmakers dropped from 62,500 to 12,500, and Japanese companies took a commanding lead in the production of watches throughout the world. The Swiss Chronological Institute had had the initial advantage because they developed quartz watches, but they gave it up by failing to exploit it fully in the world market.

In 1959, Ford Motor Company brought out the Edsel, one of the biggest mistakes in car manufacturing history. Eight years passed from the time it was conceived by the engineers and the marketers to the time it was released. The market changed completely, and when released, there was no demand for the Edsel. Ford lost more than $250 million dollars and the name Edsel became a synonym for a major marketing mistake.

Some years later, another engineer at Ford developed an idea for a minivan that would replace the station wagon. Many people at Ford, including Lee Iacocca, the president at that time, thought that the minivan had tremendous potential. But far more people at Ford, remembering the disaster with the Edsel, were afraid of making another mistake by committing to a new and untried product. If there was a real demand for a minivan, they figured, car buyers in America would be writing in and telling Ford what they wanted.

"Victory in the next war will depend on execution, not plans."

—GENERAL GEORGE PATTON

However, this scenario is seldom true. It is quite common for customers to have no idea that they want a particular product until the product is available. This is true of most high-tech products, most foods, fashion, and concepts like Federal Express and thousands of other market innovations. Often, you have no choice but to press forward in the *faith* and *confidence* that your product or service will find a ready market when you bring it out.

Lee Iacocca moved on to assume the presidency of Chrysler Corporation and turned the company around. He had a clear objective, he took aggressive action, and he concentrated on financial results. He unified the company under his command, acquired accurate market intelligence, got everyone working together proactively, secured his financial flanks, economized on operations, surprised his competition, and turned huge losses into profits in less than three years.

Once Chrysler was profitable again, the engineer at Ford who had pioneered the minivan project came to Iacocca and asked if he would be interested in looking at it again. Iacocca jumped on the project immediately, and soon thereafter Chrysler introduced into the market the first American family-style minivan, the Aerostar.

It was a huge success from the very beginning. Today, Daimler-Chrysler Corporation has almost 50 percent of the American market for minivans and has earned billions of dollars of profit from sales. No other company has been able to catch up with them. They saw an opportunity, took full advantage of it, and they exploited it to the full.

The Sales Process

For many years in selling, it was quite common to hear, "The sale begins when the customer says no." We know today, however, that the sale begins when the customer says yes.

When the customer finally agrees to buy your product or service, *that* is where the real work begins. Now you must redouble your efforts to make sure that this sale comes together and stays together.

Many people take a sale almost all of the way to closing and then lose it at the last minute. Why is this? Based on interviews with thousands of customers, we find that many customers experience a *motivation dip* immediately after agreeing to buy something. Sometimes this is called *buyer's remorse*. After the purchase, the customer begins to think of all the difficulties, problems, and uncertainties involved in using the new product or service.

It is at this point that the customer needs the greatest amount of care and attention by the sales professional. This is the moment when the customer will begin to lose heart and question her decision. This is why, at the moment that your customer decides to proceed, you must redouble your efforts to make sure you follow through with the sale.

The very best strategy in selling is to do something immediately to reassure the customer that she has made a good decision. This can be a phone call, a visit, an additional exercise in customer satisfaction or customer delight, or something else. But the more important the sale, the more important it is that you reinforce it immediately after the customer has made the decision to proceed.

Over the course of my career, I have often worked very hard to make a sale. When the customer would finally agree to proceed, I would breathe a great sigh of relief and turn my attention to other customers, or go home for the weekend. Then when I called the customer back a few days later, the person would sometimes have changed his mind completely, and I was never able to resurrect the sale. It was only when I learned about the motivation dip that customers experience that I was able to guard against this happening. It was only when I followed through to the very end of the sale that my income in sales took off. Making the sale is not enough. It is much better to follow through to the final victory.

Operation Desert Storm

Operation Desert Storm in 1991 was an example of military brilliance, utilizing and employing all of the proven principles of strategic success in warfare. Only one principle was missing; exploitation. The allies failed to drive through to Baghdad and eliminate the Iraqi government and its capability for making war again in the future.

There were several reasons for the decision not to press the war through to a final conclusion and exploit the victory over the Iraqi forces in Kuwait. But the end result was that Saddam Hussein was left in power and much of the Iraqi military capability left intact. The cost to return and finish the job will be vastly more than if the allied forces had followed through and taken advantage of their victory.

Develop Your Customers In Depth

If you don't develop customers while making the sale, trying to develop them later will cost more in time and money, and you will be less likely to succeed. A referral is worth ten or twenty times a cold call. The very best time to get a referral from a customer is immediately after the customer has bought. When customers make a buying decision, they have already gone through the process of rationalization and justification to assure themselves that this is the right thing to do. When you ask for a reference or referral at that point, customers will often encourage you to offer the same product or service to someone else they know. When you walk in on a new prospect with a referral from someone he knows, you are already most of the way toward making the sale.

From now on, when you make a sale, follow through and develop the customer in depth. Look beyond the first sale to the second, third, and even the fourth sale. Once the customer has signed on the dotted line, you should begin to think immediately about how you can sell even more products and services to this customer, the customer's company, and the customer's family or friends. Seize the advantage.

A woman who participated in one of my sales seminars used this referral process very skillfully. She made one sale to a customer who was quite pleased with her and her product. She immediately asked him for more referrals. Over the next twelve months, she tracked seventy-two additional sales from that one customer as the result of giving excellent service.

Capitalize on a Market Niche

Similar customers have similar motivations and similar needs. If you can identify a particular customer in a particular industry, position, occupation, or situation and then sell your product or service to that customer, you will have learned something vital and important. You will have learned a lot about how to sell to other people who are similar to the customer with whom you have just closed the deal.

Let's say you make a sale to a person who works in a particular industry. To make that sale, you will have had to learn a great deal about that industry and how it functions. Now you have *a knowledge base*. Now you can take that same skill and knowledge and turn to another individual in the same industry and capitalize on what you have learned. You can take advantage of your ability to sell in that type of market.

Your knowledge of the way your customer does business is valuable. It can be your stock in trade as a salesperson. The more you know about the functioning of your customer's industry or field, the easier it is for you to sell to that particular type of customer. You are much more capable of identifying and solving problems or satisfying needs with what you sell.

Specialize in a Particular Industry

A friend of mine joined the life insurance industry in sales some years ago. He concluded very quickly that people who had *more* money were better prospects than people who had less money. He also saw, of course, that doctors and other medical professionals had a high, consistent, and predictable level of income. Therefore, if he could sell to medical professionals, he could create quite a business for himself.

But instead of calling doctors and dentists out of the yellow pages, he began a detailed research project that ultimately took two years to complete. He learned everything he could about the way medical professionals structure their finances. He read books and attended medical conventions. He interviewed countless medical professionals and talked to other people who had medical professionals as clients.

Eventually he was asked to speak on financial planning to groups of doctors. Soon he came to be recognized as a financial planning and insurance expert for people who were earning their living in one of the medical professions.

As his reputation for expertise in this area spread, business began to flow to him like a river. He was successful because he had used the twin ideas of first seeking out an opportunity area, and then exploiting it to the full by becoming an expert in that area. He didn't stop when he identified a market. He followed through to find the best way to reach that market.

People always want to buy from the experts. Customers always want to deal with the individuals and organizations they feel are the best in the industry. When you focus on becoming an expert in a particular field, more and more people in that field will want to do business with you.

Higher Quality Leads to More Sales

According to PIMS Studies at Harvard University, companies that are recognized as the highest quality providers in their markets are also the companies that sell the most and sell the easiest. They can charge more than their competitors, and they earn the highest profit margins.

The highest rated companies in terms of quality also grow the most rapidly, attract and keep the best people, and pay the best salaries. The "quality ranking" of a company is the most important single determining factor in the success of a company, and in the success of the individuals who sell and work for that company.

Thousands of consumers have been interviewed over the years and asked for their definitions of "quality." Their responses show that the quality of a company is measured and determined by two factors. The first factor is the quality of the product itself. The second is the manner in which the product was sold and delivered.

It is not only the product or service that the company offers, but the temperament, mood, and personality of the people who deliver the product or service that, combined, give a company its quality ranking in a given industry. The company needs a great product or service, but more important, it needs to follow through with good marketing, service, and delivery.

Here is a good question for you, then: What is your quality ranking in your marketplace? Imagine that your company is one of ten major companies offering the same product or service in your marketplace. Intuitively, what do you think your quality ranking would be if customers were surveyed and asked to rank your company on a scale of one to ten against your competitors? This ranking largely determines your levels of sales and profitability.

Determine How Your Customers Define Quality. Before you can exploit an advantage you have over the competition, you need to first determine whether your customers value that particular advantage. Ask your customers how they define the word "quality." What words do they use? How do they determine that one product or service is of higher or lower quality than another? The greater clarity you have about how your customers define quality as it relates to your offerings, the more capable you will become of improving in those areas that your customers consider important.

According to Phil Crosby in his book *Quality Is Free,* the general meaning of quality is that, "Your product or service does what you say it will do and continues to do it." The percentage of the time that your product or service delivers on the promises that you make to sell it is the quality rating. "Zero defects" means that your product or service fulfills its promises 100 percent of the time. This is what every customer is looking for.

Once you know how your customers define quality and you have decided to improve your quality ranking, you then develop a strategy and make a plan to improve in those areas that are important to your customers. You decide what you are going to do to improve your customer's perception of your organization and of the products and services you sell.

For example, do customers consider *speed of delivery* a factor in quality? If they do, commit yourself to delivering your products faster than they are being delivered today. Do your customers consider *convenience of use* a quality factor? What about speed of responsiveness or politeness on the telephone? Do your customers value the importance of *accurate billing* and quick replies to questions with regard to cost and price? Do your customers value *follow-up service and support*? Focus on improving in those areas that are most likely to determine a buying decision.

Remember the 80/20 Rule. Twenty percent of the things you do will account for 80 percent of the reasons your customers buy from you. Twenty percent of your features and benefits will determine whether they continue to buy from you and recommend you to their friends. You must know for sure what items are in the top 20 percent.

There is a danger here, though. You could make the mistake of concentrating on becoming extremely good and efficient in an area related to your product or service that your customers don't care about at all. You could be draining vital time and resources away from improving in the one or two areas that could make an enormous difference in the perception of your customers.

Once you find out what your customers want and need and are willing to pay for, you should exploit this to the full. You should take every opportunity to not only improve in those critical areas but also to advertise, promote, and sell to other customers by emphasizing how good you really are in those areas that mean so much to them.

Why Do They Buy from You? To fully take advantage of your position in the market, determine what makes you special. You must be continually asking your customers why it is that they buy from you. What is it that they like the most about what you do? Why is it that customers prefer to deal with you rather than your competitors? The answers to these questions represent your greatest opportunities for exploitation and development in your marketplace.

A Rolex watch can cost many thousands of dollars. But Rolex is not sold as a timepiece. Rolex is sold as a status symbol. Rolex has managed to position itself as the watch you wear to tell other people that you have "arrived." Wearing a Rolex watch makes a statement to the people around you that you are successful and prosperous. And people are willing to pay many thousands of dollars to make this statement.

Why is it, *exactly,* that people buy your product or service? How can you exploit and develop that market advantage to leapfrog ahead of your competitors?

Operation Barbarossa

Adolph Hitler launched Operation Barbarossa against the Soviet Union in June of 1941 with three million crack German troops supported by tanks and motorized infantry. Three German Army Groups (North, Center, and South), perhaps the best fighting forces in the world at that time, rolled across Russia, overwhelming the Russian forces opposing them. They were virtually unstoppable.

The overall objective of the campaign was to take Moscow, which was the central hub of the entire country for communications, railroads, and highways. If the Germans could take it, Russia would be defeated and knocked out of the war.

The German armies, having achieved almost complete surprise, pushed across Russia, destroying and scattering all resistance in their way. In the first three months of the campaign, more than 1,500,000 prisoners had been taken. In Moscow, Stalin and his government were preparing to evacuate and flee the capital. The end was in sight.

As the Germans advanced, they saw a great opportunity to encircle and destroy the sixty-nine divisions and one million men of Marshall Budyenny's southwest front and to take Kiev. Hitler immediately ordered the three army groups to work in concert to cut off, surround, and eliminate these Russian troops as a fighting force in what is known as the Kiev Encirclement. (This strategy of surrounding enemy forces is called the Cannae Principle, because it was used by Hannibal to encircle and destroy the Roman Army at Cannae in Italy in 216 B.C.)

In order to turn their attention to this encircling movement, the German armies halted their advance on Moscow. The encircled Russians fought bitterly but unsuccessfully to break through the German infantry. But because of their fierce resistance, the battle lasted from late August until early October. Kiev fell to the Germans at the end of September, and an additional 600,000 Russians had been taken prisoner by October. So the Germans achieved victory, but at a great cost.

The Germans resumed their advance on Moscow, but it was now too late. Even though German advance forces penetrated to within ten miles of the outskirts of the city, their supply lines had been stretched too far, and the Russian winter, for which they were ill-prepared, was coming on. The Russians counterattacked, and the Germans were forced to withdraw into defensible positions for the winter.

By the spring, the Russians had rearmed and reequipped new armies recruited from east of the Ural Mountains. Their factories produced hundreds of tanks and fighter aircraft. As a result, the Germans were never able to take Moscow and conquer the Soviet Union. Their attempts to take Leningrad in the north and Stalingrad in the south also met with failure. By 1943, it was clear that Germany could not win the war in Russia. Time now turned against them. The failure to follow through in 1941 cost them the war.

Hitler saw an opportunity to attack one division and quickly took it. Fortunately for the Russians, this opportunity was actually a distraction from his main, and more important, objective of taking Moscow.

Move Quickly on Opportunities, but Stay on Track

Opportunities are like windows. They open and close, sometimes quite quickly. When you have an idea for something you can do to be more successful, take action immediately, but make sure the opportunity supports your objectives. Hitler moved quickly on an opportunity, but he didn't understand that the opportunity would prevent him from reaching his primary objective. When you get a recommendation or a referral, call that person as fast as you can get to a phone. When you read about a new idea or concept, try it out as fast as you can. When a window of opportunity opens for you, dive through it quickly, because it will close again just as fast as it opened in the first place.

Bill Gates and Paul Allen started Microsoft Corporation in Bellevue, Washington. In the early years they struggled, as all entrepreneurs do. One day Gates was invited by IBM to submit a proposal for an operating system for the new personal computer that IBM was developing. Microsoft did not yet have an operating system, nor did it have time to develop the type of system that IBM wanted. But Bill Gates said, "Sure, right away!" He then began looking around for someone, anyone, who had already done the complicated work of developing a computer operating system.

There was a small company in Seattle that had developed an operating system and had even tried to sell it to IBM. After some negotiating, he bought it from them for $50,000. This company had invested an enormous amount of time and energy in developing the system but could not develop the market. Gates did not have the system, but he had the potential market.

This was a match that worked out perfectly for both Microsoft and IBM. The system became Microsoft Disc Operating System, commonly known as MS-DOS. It evolved into Windows and is now built into 90 percent of the world's personal computers. By seizing an opportunity and running with it—and figuring out how to make it work as he went along—Bill Gates laid the groundwork for becoming the richest man in the world.

The Principle of Exploitation in Personal Success

There has never been a better time, and there have never been more opportunities than right now, for you to achieve your goals and objectives—faster and easier than ever before. You are surrounded by opportunities and possibilities that have never existed until now. You can make breakthroughs today that will enable you to accomplish more in the next few years than most people accomplish in a lifetime.

But opportunities usually come disguised in work clothes, i.e., as hard work. They may be all around you, but to maximize them, you have to follow up and follow through with each one. You have to exploit them to the full. Bruce Barton once wrote, "Most successful men have not achieved their distinction by having some new talent or opportunity presented to them. They have developed the opportunity that was at hand."

It is such a tragedy to see how many people work so hard and get 95 percent of their goal achieved only to back off, slow down, and relax. Then, for reasons completely outside their control, the goal slips out of their grasp and they find themselves losing everything they've put into it.

George Cecil said it well "On the plains of hesitation bleach the bones of countless millions who, at the dawn of victory, sat down to wait, and waiting, died."

Acres of Diamonds

Perhaps the most widely disseminated story ever told regarding opportunities and possibilities and the need to exploit them is Russell Conwell's famous talk, "Acres of Diamonds." In this talk, which he gave more than 5,000 times during his lifetime, Conwell emphasized that you do not have to go somewhere else to find your great opportunity. It frequently lies close at hand.

The story he told was that of an African farmer who sold his farm and went off into Africa looking for diamonds. He never found any. After years of frustration and failure, he finally threw himself into the ocean and drowned.

Meanwhile, the new farmer back on the same land found that his farm was actually covered with acres of diamonds. But the diamonds looked like rough pieces of rock before they were cut and shaped and polished. The old farmer had been sitting on acres of diamonds, but he had not recognized them.

Your acres of diamonds lie under your own feet as well. But they are disguised as your special talents and abilities, your education and experience, your friends and contacts. Your greatest possibilities probably lie close at hand: in your current job, your present business or industry, and in your existing market. Your job is to identify them and then to exploit them. Take advantage of every opportunity for service you can find.

"Start where you are," Robert Collier said. "Distant fields always look greener, but opportunity lies right where you are."

Turning Defeat Into Victory

To view the Gallipoli Campaign from the Turkish point of view, though the Turks were taken by surprise and were at first unprepared to defend themselves, they were able to turn their defeat into victory by taking advantage of the opportunity of time. *Think and Grow Rich* author Napoleon Hill found that successful men and women are masters at turning defeat into

---

"A wise man will make more opportunities than he finds."

—FRANCIS BACON

---

victory. He summed up his views with these words: "Opportunity often comes disguised in the form of misfortune or temporary defeat." And he added an observation and an exhortation: "Within every setback or disappointment lies the seed of an equal or greater advantage or benefit. Your job is to find it." To find your opportunities for exploitation and development, look around you. Look within yourself. What are your unique talents and abilities? What is it that the world needs that you are uniquely suited to give it? What is it that you do better than anyone else?

Look within yourself for your own "personal" acres of diamonds. What has been most responsible for your success in life to date? What do you most enjoy doing? What do you do easily and well that is often difficult for others?

Look back over your life. What activities and accomplishments have given you the greatest amount of satisfaction and happiness? The answers to these questions will indicate where you can develop and exploit your opportunities to the fullest in the future.

The fact is that you may be surrounded by opportunities that only need to be developed and exploited. You must recognize them, seize them, and take advantage of them. Once you get an opportunity, you must run with it and follow it on to completion. You must exploit it fully. And you must do it quickly and well.

Do All You Can

When a farmer has sown the seeds and cultivated the crop, and then fall comes and the crop is ready, how much does the farmer harvest? The answer is, "All he can!"

How much do you sell? All you can! How long do you persist? As long as it takes! How much do you develop and exploit every opportunity that comes to you? As much as it takes to make it successful!

Luck is always a matter of *probabilities*. The more different things you try, the more likely it is that you will triumph. Luck comes from intelligently trying as many different things as possible. It comes from learning as many different subjects as possible. It comes from accepting feedback and self-correcting as quickly as possible, and persisting with indomitable willpower until you finally break through.

The good news is that your chances of great success are extremely high if you know what you want, put your whole heart into it, and then persist until you succeed. Once you get your opportunity or breakthrough, that is the time to redouble your efforts and increase the pressure, rather than sit back and relax.

Something Always Happens

In wartime England, 1941, during the darkest days of World War II, Winston Churchill was urged to seek an accommodation with the Germans—to make peace. This he refused to do. When he was confronted with the fact that the Germans had overwhelming military superiority in Europe and the Americans had made it clear that they would not get involved again in a land war in Europe, why was it that Churchill refused to seek some kind of peace agreement to end the war?

Churchill said, "Something will happen to bring America into the war, and that will turn the tide."

When he was asked why he was so confident that something like that would happen, he said, "Because I have studied history and history shows that if you persist long enough, something always happens!"

Sometimes *luck* comes as the result of your persisting with what you are doing until the tables finally turn and you get your chance. It seems that a streak of bad luck is often followed by a streak of good luck. A sales slump is often followed by a sales boom. It is therefore essential that, at the time of greatest discouragement, you redouble your efforts and recommit yourself to persist with your whole heart.

Opportunities multiply as they are seized. The more you take advantage of opportunities, the more opportunities open up for you. As you move toward your goal, you begin to see possibilities that were invisible before you began moving forward.

Look for Opportunities Everywhere

Look around you at all the possible opportunities in your environment that will help you achieve victory. Of all the different things that you could possibly be doing, what is the 20 percent of your activities that could potentially represent 80 percent of your success? What are the major customer, product, service, or promotional breakthroughs that you could achieve that could have the biggest impact on your business or your sales activities?

High sales in your business begins with differentiating yourself in a meaningful way from your competitors. More business is the result of becoming very, very good at what you do. Market success is based on your achieving a competitive advantage, an area of excellence where you are superior to your competition.

The questions are always the same: "What is it that you do, or can do, in an excellent fashion? Where can you gain and keep market superiority? What is the one thing that you can do right now, that can make the greatest single difference to your success in the future?"

The Military Principle of Exploitation Revisited

Your ability to follow up and follow through on your ideas and opportunities will determine how high you climb and how far you go. Once you have a breakthrough or an advantage, you must exploit it to the full.

In business, you must identify your greatest strengths and focus all your marketing and sales on selling more and more where those strengths are most appreciated. You must identify your best opportunities for the future and commit your resources to exploiting them in every way possible. You must be persistent and unrelenting in getting the very most out of every benefit you have or can develop.

In your personal life, you must fully develop and exploit your special talents and abilities. You must become absolutely excellent at doing those things that can make the greatest contribution to the achievement of your most important goals.

When doors open for you, as they will, you must be prepared to plunge through them. You must be willing to take intelligent risks to realize the potential of each advantageous situation, and to realize your full potential as a person.

The Military Principles of Strategy Revisited

You can become extremely successful by doing what other top military leaders and business executives have done before you. By applying the principles of military strategy to your life and work, you can learn to think and act faster and more effectively than anyone else around you. When you practice the critical thinking tools used by the greatest leaders in history, you can dramatically increase your effectiveness and improve your results in everything you do.

  1. **The Principle of the Objective.** Decide exactly what it is you want, write it down, make a plan, and then work on your plan every single day. Develop and maintain

absolute clarity regarding your goals and objectives, and make sure everyone involved knows what they are.

2. **The Principle of the Offensive.** Become an intensely action-oriented person. Throw your whole heart into what you are doing. Become a moving target. All great battles are won on the offensive by taking aggressive forward action.

3. **The Principle of the Mass.** Focus single-mindedly on one thing, the most important thing, and stay with it until it is done. Bring all your powers to bear on achieving your most important single goal or accomplishing the most important single objective in your work or personal life. Always focus on the one or two things that you can do that can make all the difference. Don't waste your precious energies on lower-value activities. As Goethe said, "The things that matter most must never be at the mercy of things that matter least."

4. **The Principle of Maneuver.** Be fast on your feet. Try something new. Try it again and then try something else. Look for ways to do things differently, to come at your problems and opportunities from a different angle than the average person. Be willing to consider the possibility that you could be wrong in your most cherished assumptions or your most habitual behaviors.

5. **The Principle of Intelligence.** Learn all you can about your business and your industry, especially the plans and actions of your competitors. Get the facts. You can never have too much information or too many ideas. Become very good at what you do. Read, listen to audio

programs, and take seminars and courses regularly. Ask questions, listen carefully, and make notes. One good idea is all you need to change your life.

6. **The Principle of Concerted Action.** Learn to work well with other people. Leverage the talents and skills of others to help you achieve your goals. Associate with positive people who are going somewhere with their lives. Always look for ways to help others achieve their goals, and they will always be willing to help you achieve yours.

7. **The Principle of Unity of Command.** Be a leader. Take charge. Seize the initiative. Make a decision, then another, then another. Learn from your decisions; accept feedback and self-correct. Remember that you are where you are and what you are because of yourself. You are in charge of your own life and your own future. Take command!

8. **The Principle of Simplicity.** Continually look for ways to simplify your life and your work. Cut out all useless activities. Reduce complexity at every opportunity. Make a decision today to delegate, eliminate, consolidate, out-source, and discontinue activities that no longer contribute significant value to the achievement of your most important goals and objectives.

9. **The Principle of Security.** Guard against losses and reversals. Insure against any emergency. Put aside cash reserves. Protect your main markets. Take excellent care of your most important customers. Treasure your most valuable people. Think ahead about what could possibly

go wrong, and then make provisions to ensure that those things don't happen. Take nothing for granted.

10. **The Principle of Economy.** Minimize your costs. Continually seek ways to achieve your objectives with a minimum expenditure of time and money. Make a decision to become financially independent in the course of your working lifetime, and organize your financial activities so that you achieve your goal on schedule. Save regularly and invest carefully.

11. **The Principle of Surprise.** Do the unexpected. Always be looking for newer, faster, easier, cheaper ways to accomplish the same objective. The only constant in life today is change, and the rate of change is accelerating. Your ability to be creative and innovative, to find different ways to serve your customers better and faster, is the key to your breaking through all the barriers to success in your industry.

12. **The Principle of Exploitation.** Follow up and follow through. Make a commitment today to fulfill your full potential as a person. Decide right now that you are going to become everything you are capable of becoming. When you get an opportunity, throw your whole heart into taking full advantage of it, and never, never give up.

As you incorporate these twelve military principles into your life, remember that every extraordinary achievement is usually an accumulation of hundreds and thousands of ordinary achievements that no one ever sees or appreciates. These accumulated achievements can add up to significantly more money and rewards for you if you follow the 1,000 percent formula. The 1,000 percent formula is based on the strategy of continuous betterment, or the Kaizen Strategy. Just as it has worked to create giant world industries, it can work for you.

The 1,000 Percent Formula

When I was 30 years old, after a series of ups and downs, sometimes making more and sometimes making less, my income for the year was $14,400. Twelve years later, my income was over $1,500,000, an increase of more than 100 times!

What happened in between was that I put together a formula for income improvement that I followed every day, every week, and every year thereafter. Although there were fluctuations in my income over the years, it continued to increase, as long as I followed the formula that I am about to share with you.

The 1,000 percent formula is based on the discovery that it is possible for you to increase your income by ten times over the next ten years. Most people are incredulous and amazed at the very idea of *doubling* their income over the next ten years, much less increasing it by ten times. However, I have shared this formula with people all over the world. I have never had anyone come back and tell me that it didn't work. If anything, this formula is conservative, as you will see for yourself.

It is very simple. By following the seven-step formula listed below, you can increase your productivity, performance, output and eventually, your income by one tenth of 1 percent each day.

One tenth of 1 percent is an improvement of 1/1000th in your overall effectiveness and efficiency in the course of a 24-hour day.

Is it possible for you, if you really *wanted* to, if you were determined to, to increase your overall productivity and performance by 1/1,000th in a 24-hour day?

You will have to admit that 1/10th of 1 percent, or 1/1000th improvement over the course of a day is not very much. In fact, if you were just to plan your day a little better and concentrate on your highest value tasks a bit more, you would probably increase your productivity by 50 percent in a single day, rather than less a mere 1/1,000th!

If you increase your productivity, performance, and output by 1/10th of 1 percent per day, five days a week, and you don't improve at all on the weekends, you will improve by approximately ½ of 1 percent per week. This is a 1/200th improvement every five days. Again, could you do this if your life depended on it? What if your *future* depended upon it? Of course you could!

If you increase your productivity, performance, and output by ½ of 1 percent per week and you do this every week throughout the year, at the end of the year, even without the compounding effects that will occur, you will be producing 26 percent more than you were twelve months earlier. Is it possible for a hard working, determined, ambitious individual like you to upgrade your productivity, performance, and output by 26 percent over a one year period?

The fact is that you could probably do much better if you really wanted to. But 26 percent over the course of 12 months, one day at a time, is eminently achievable. This is the principle of continuous improvement in action.

Every improvement in one area leads to small improvements in other areas. Very much like the miracle of compound interest, as you get better and better in some things that you do, you seem to get better in other things as well.

A 26 percent improvement each year, compounded, would lead to a doubling of your productivity, performance, and output in less than three years and an increase of 1,004 percent in your productivity, performance, and earning ability in ten years.

Some years ago, in Portland, Oregon, I shared this formula with a group of young salesmen. Seven years later I was visiting Portland again and one of those salesmen approached me. I still remembered him. He said, "Brian, I have been practicing your 1,000 percent formula every day, without fail, for seven years. And it doesn't work."

I asked him, "How do you mean?"

He smiled and with great delight he told me, "It didn't take ten years to increase my income ten times. It has only been seven years. As of this February, my income was ten times what it was when you first taught me that formula."

Seven Steps to Success

Here is the seven-step formula. Each of these principles is so powerful that one of them alone could increase your productivity, performance, output, and income by 1000 percent. When you practice all seven principles every day, your results will increase at a faster rate than you can currently imagine.

Step One: Arise a little earlier and spend the first 30–60 minutes of each morning reading something educational, inspirational, or motivational. The first hour is the "rudder of the day." Invest the first hour in yourself, in reading and preparing your mind for the day. This alone will give you a 1,000 percent gain over ten years.

Step Two: Rewrite your major goals each day in a spiral note-book, in the present tense, exactly as if they had already been achieved. This exercise takes three to five minutes and it pro-grams your subconscious, your superconscious, and your retic-ular activating system for the rest of the day. By continually refocusing your mental powers on your most important goals, you will be amazed at how many of those goals you achieve, and how fast you achieve them.

Step Three: Plan every day in advance, preferably the night before. Make out a detailed list of everything that you have to do the next day—before you go to bed. This allows your sub-conscious mind to work on the list while you sleep. Often, when you wake up in the morning, you will have ideas and insights that will enable you to complete your tasks and achieve your goals even faster than you thought possible.

Step Four: Set priorities on your list and always concentrate single-mindedly on the most valuable use of your time. This practice alone will increase your productivity, performance, and output by 1,000 percent over ten years, or sooner. No mat-ter what happens, like a gyroscope, keep coming back to your most important task and stay at it until it is complete.

Step Five: Listen to audio programs in your car. Turn your car into a "university on wheels." Never let your automobile be running without educational audio programs playing.

By listening to audio programs as you drive, you can get an additional 500 to 1,000 hours of concentrated instruction. As you move from place to place in your mobile classroom, con-tinually feed your mind with great ideas that can help you to improve your life and work, and achieve your goals. Don't waste time listening to music.

Step Six: Ask the two magic questions after every experience, whether it is successful or unsuccessful:

1. **What did I do right?** Even if you made a mistake, or something did not work out well, immediately analyze the situation by identifying all the things that you did *right* in that situation. This analysis prepares your mind to repeat the correct things you did when you find yourself in a similar situation.

2. **What would I do differently?** If you had this situation to do over again, how would you change or improve it in some way? The more answers you have to this question, the better you will perform the next time a similar situation arises.

These two questions are amazing! The more you ask and answer these questions, the more you learn from every experience and the faster you move ahead. These two questions alone can give you your 1,000 percent increase over the next ten years.

Step Seven: Treat every person you meet like a million-dollar customer, starting at home with the members of your family. As you go through the day, treat everyone you meet as if that person has the ability to buy one million dollars of your product or service, or to steer such a buyer to you.

Thomas Carlyle once wrote, "You can tell a big person by the way he treats little people." Ann Landers wrote, "The true mark of character is how you treat a person who can't do you any good." When you habitually treat people as though they are valuable and important, not only will this have a positive effect on your personality, it will open doors and create opportunities for you that you cannot today imagine.

Summing Up

As we move into the twenty-first century, we are entering into the "Golden Age" of mankind. We are entering into a period where more people will accomplish more than has ever been accomplished or dreamed of in all the history of humanity.

There are no limits on what you can accomplish except the limits that you place in your own mind. It doesn't matter where you are coming from; all that really matters is where you are *going*. And where you are going is limited only by your own imagination. As Shakespeare said, "What is past is prologue."

Perhaps the most important thing to remember in the weeks and months ahead is that *you can learn anything you need to learn to achieve any goal you set for yourself.* You can develop any skill or quality that you need, to become the kind of person that you need to be, to achieve any success that you desire. Theodore Roosevelt said that the key to success is, "Do what you can, with what you have, where you are."

Anything that anyone else has done, you can probably do as well. Any goals that others have achieved, you can achieve as well, within reason. There are no real limits on what you can do, have, and be when you take complete control over your life and your future destiny. When you resolve right here and right now to apply these principles of strategy to everything you do, you will achieve victories beyond anything you have ever accomplished. You will become unstoppable.

Brian Tracy's Focal Point Advanced Coaching and Mentoring Program

Brian Tracy offers a personal group coaching program in San Diego for successful entrepreneurs, self-employed professionals, and top salespeople who want to move to the next level in their careers and their personal lives. In this program, you learn how to double your productivity, simplify your life, and double your time off.

Coaching sessions are small and personal, with ample opportunity for interaction and brainstorming with other successful people. During the program, you meet with Brian Tracy one full day every three months. As a result of a series of powerful self-analysis exercises, you identify those things you do best. You then learn how to excel in your most profitable activities.

You learn how to develop your own personal strategic plan, how to implement your plan with daily, weekly, and monthly goals, and how to update your plan as you move forward.

In addition, you learn how to delegate, outsource, and eliminate tasks and activities that contribute very little to the achievement of your most important business and career goals.

If you qualify for this program (minimum income $100,000 per year), you will learn how to apply the **Focal Point Process** to every part of your work and personal life, and you will make more progress in one year than someone else might make in ten.

Focal Point Advanced Coaching Program by Telephone

Brian Tracy International also offers an intensive 12-week advanced coaching program by telephone that you can take in the convenience of your home or office. You work with an expert coach who has had many years of experience in helping successful people get the most out of themselves and their lives.

You receive a detailed 12-part, 410-page study guide, plus a complete outline of the program on audio for your review. Each week, you complete one session and answer several questions in preparation for your telephone meeting with your coach. After each coaching session you then develop an action plan for the coming week that keeps you moving forward.

At each stage, your coach will guide you and advise you to help you realize more and more of your potential. At the end of 12 weeks, you will be performing on a new high level of effectiveness and personal satisfaction.

For more information or to apply for the next live or personal coaching program by phone, visit www.briantracy.com and click on Coaching, or phone 858-481-2977. We will send you a complete information package. Or write to Brian Tracy at Brian Tracy International, 420 Stevens Avenue, Solana Beach, CA, 92075.

Bibliography

Military Reference Sources

Alexander, Bevin. *How Great Generals Win.* Norton, 1993.

Axelrod, Allan. *Patton on Leadership: Strategic Lessons for Corporate Warfare.* Prentice Hall, 2001.

Chandler, David, ed. *The Military Maxims of Napoleon.* Translated by Sir George C. D'Aguilar. Greenhill, 1987.

Charlton, James. *The Military Quotation Book: More Than 600 of the Best Quotations About War, Courage, Combat, Victory, and Defeat.* St. Martin's, 2002.

Clausewitz, Karl von. *On War.* Translated and edited by Michael Howard and Peter Paret. Princeton University Press, 1976.

Cohen, Elliot A. and John Gooch. *Military Misfortunes: The Anatomy of Failure in War.* Free Press, 1990.

Cohen, William A. *Wisdom of the Generals.* Prentice Hall, 2001.

Cowley, Robert, and Geoffrey Parker, eds. *The Reader's Companion to Military History.* Houghton-Mifflin, 1996.

Creasy, Sir Edward Shepherd. *Fifteen Decisive Battles of the World: From Marathon to Waterloo.* Dorset, 1987.

Department of the Army. *Field Manual 100-5, Operations, Headquarters.* June 1993.

D'Este, Carlo. *Patton: A Genius for War.* HarperCollins, 1995.

Eggenberger, David. *An Encyclopedia of Battles: Accounts of Over 1560 Battles From 1479 B.C. to the Present.* Dover, 1985.

Farago, Ladislaw. *Patton: Ordeal and Triumph.* Barker, 1966.

Flexner, James Thomas. *Washington: The Indispensable Man.* Little, Brown, 1969.

Foote, Shelby. *The Civil War: A Narrative.* 3 vols. Random House, 1958–1974.

Freeman, Douglas Southall. *Lee.* Scribner's, 1961.

Fuller, J. F. C. *The Decisive Battles of the Western World and Their Influence on History.* 2 vols. Hunter, 1988.

Fuller, J. F. C. *The Generalship of Alexander the Great.* Da Capo Press, 1989.

Green, Peter. *Alexander of Macedon 356–323 B.C.: A Historical Biography.* University of California Press, 1991.

Green, Robert. *The 48 Laws of Power.* Viking, 1998.

Hanson, Victor Davis. *Carnage and Culture: Landmark Battles in the Rise of Western Power.* Doubleday, 2001.

Hastings, Max, ed. *The Oxford Book of Military Anecdotes.* Oxford University Press, 1985.

Keegan, John. *The Face of Battle.* Viking, 1976.

Keegan, John, *The First World War.* Knopf, 1999.

Liddell Hart, B. H. *Great Captains Unveiled.* Greenhill, 1927.

Lucas, James Sidney, ed. *Command: A Historical Dictionary of Military Leaders.* Military Press, 1988.

Luvaas, Jay, ed. and trans. *Napoleon on the Art of War.* Simon and Schuster, 1999.

McPherson, James M. *The Battle Cry of Freedom: The Civil War Era.* Oxford University Press, 1988.

Musashi, Miyamoto. *A Book of Five Rings.* Translated by G. H. Mendell. Viking, 1982.

Patton, George S. Jr., *War as I Knew It.* Houghton Mifflin, 1947.

Plutarch. *Selected Lives and Essays.* Walter J. Black, 1951.

Pratt, Fletcher. *The Battles That Changed History.* Doubleday, 1956.

Schom, Alan. *Napoleon Bonaparte: A Biography.* Harper-Collins, 1997.

Schwarzkopf, H. Norman. *It Doesn't Take a Hero.* Bantam, 1992.

Solzhenitsyn, Aleksander. *August 1914.* Translated by Harry T. Willets. Farrar, Straus, and Giroux, 1989.

Sun Tzu. *The Art of War.* Translated by Samuel B. Griffith. Oxford University Press, 1984.

Wilcken, Ulrich. *Alexander the Great.* Norton, 1967.

Index

About the Author

Brian Tracy is one of America's top business speakers, a best-selling author, and one of the leading consultants and trainers on personal and professional development in the world today. He has started, built, managed, or turned around twenty-two different businesses in diverse industries. Brian addresses 250,000 people each year on subjects ranging from Personal Success and Leadership to Managerial Effectiveness, Creativity, and Sales. He has written twenty-six books, including *Focal Point* (AMACOM), *Maximum Achievement*, and *The 100 Absolutely Unbreakable Laws of Business Success*, and has produced more than 300 audio and video learning programs. Much of his work has been translated into other languages and is being used in thirty-five countries.

Brian has consulted with more than 500 companies—IBM, McDonnell Douglas, and The Million Dollar Round Table among them—and has trained more than 2,000,000 people personally. His ideas are proven, practical, and fast-acting. His readers and seminar participants learn a series of techniques and strategies that they can use immediately to get better results in their lives and careers.